MY COSTUME BOOK

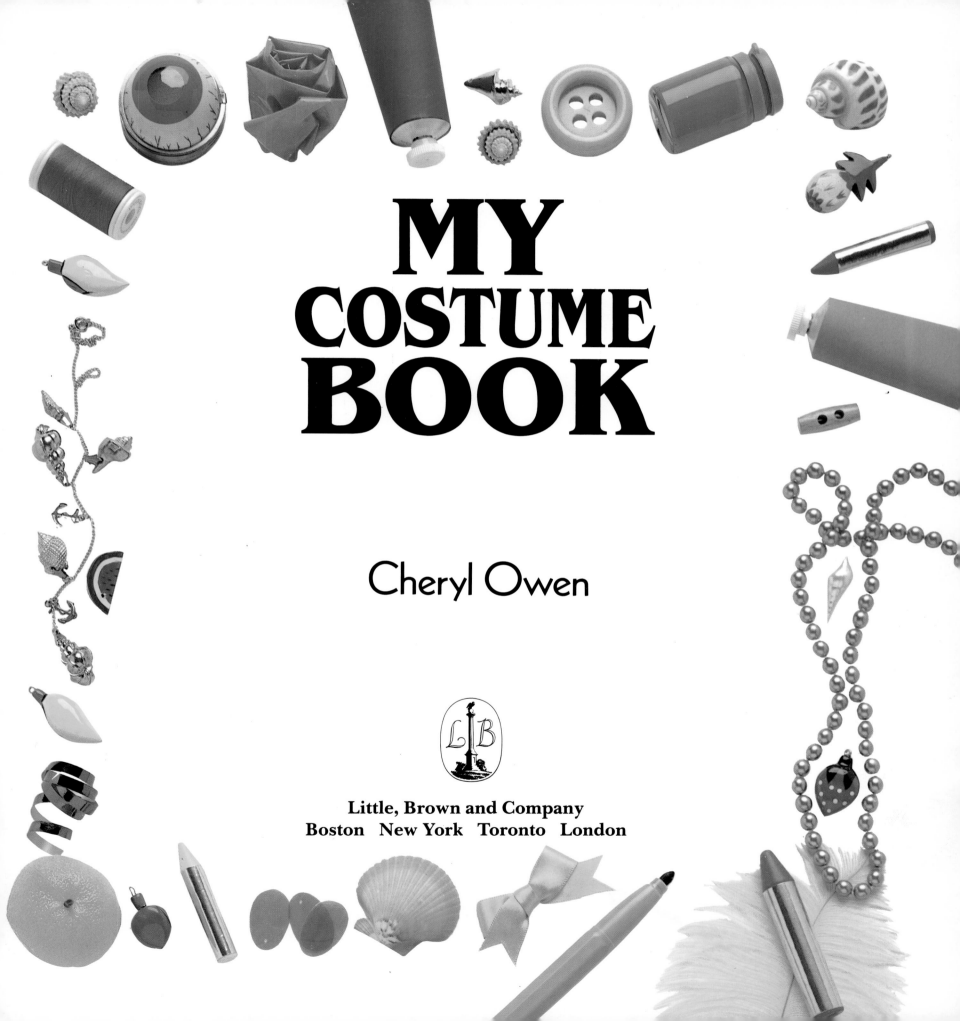

MY
COSTUME
BOOK

Cheryl Owen

Little, Brown and Company
Boston   New York   Toronto   London

First North American Edition 1995

ISBN: 0-316-67742-6

Library of Congress Catalog Card Number 94-74215

Produced by Salamander Books Limited, 129-137 York Way,
London N7 9LG, England

10 9 8 7 6 5 4 3 2

CREDITS

Photographer: Jonathan Pollock
Illustrator: Teri Gower
Character illustrator: Jo Gapper
Diagram artist: Malcolm Porter
Typeset by: SX Composing, Essex
Color separation by: P & W Graphics, Pte., Singapore

Published simultaneously in Canada by
Little, Brown & Company (Canada) Limited

Printed in Italy

The publishers would like to thank Kim Clarke, educational craft and textiles consultant, for her help and advice in compiling this book.

CONTENTS

INTRODUCTION

This colorful and imaginative book is packed with costumes for you to make, each one with easy-to-follow instructions and step-by-step pictures to help you. Get together with your friends and make the Strongman, Crazy Clown, and Friendly Lion outfits for a circus theme party, or the Vampire, Wicked Witch, and Little Devil for a spooky Halloween party.

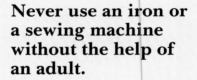

BEFORE YOU BEGIN
- Check with an adult before starting any project; you might need some help.
- Read the instructions all the way through before you begin.
- Start by gathering together all the items you will need.
- Cover your work surface with newspaper or an old cloth.
- Protect your clothes with an apron or by covering up with an old shirt.

WHEN YOU HAVE FINISHED
- Put everything away. Store special pens, paints, glue, pins, needles, and thread in old boxes, cookie tins, or ice cream containers.
- Wash paintbrushes, and remember to put the caps back on pens, paints, and glue containers.

SAFETY FIRST!
Use common sense when working with anything sharp or hot. You will be able to make most of the projects in this book by yourself, but sometimes you will need the help of an adult. Keep an eye out for SAFETY TIPS. They appear on those projects with which you'll need help.

Never use an iron or a sewing machine without the help of an adult.

Be very careful when using needles, pins, or sharp scissors.

Please remember the basic rules of safety:
- Never leave scissors open or lying around where smaller children can reach them.
- Always stick needles and pins into a pincushion or a scrap of cloth when you are not using them.
- Never use an iron, sharp scissors, or a sewing machine without the help or supervision of an adult.

MATERIALS

Before you buy any materials to make a costume, check at home with an adult first. You may find some old clothes or fabric scraps to use.

Ask your family and friends for old clothes that you can adapt for your outfits, or look in used-clothing stores for hats, clothes, belts, shoes, and other useful items. Start to collect button, beads, ribbon, and braid that might come in handy for decorating your costumes.

Some items, such as glitter paints, sticky-backed plastic, and acrylic paints, will need to be bought from a craft supplier or a department store. When thick wire is needed, bonsai tree wire, which can be bought at garden centers, is best because it is very thick but can be bent into shape easily. Floral wire, which is available at florists or craft shops, can be used when fine wire is needed.

USING PATTERNS

At the back of the book, you will find the patterns you will need to make many of the costumes in the book. To find out how to copy a pattern, follow the step-by-step instructions given with each project. Some of the patterns are shown as reduced diagrams with measurements. To find out how to draw the correct size pattern piece onto paper, follow the instructions for Making a Paper Pattern on page 8.

Once you have gained confidence making some of the costumes featured in this book, you can go on to create your own designs. If you enjoy drawing, try making up your own patterns and designs freehand.

GROWN-UPS TAKE NOTE

Every costume in *My Costume Book* has been designed to be simple to make, with satisfying results. However, some potentially dangerous items such as irons and sharp scissors are needed for some projects. Your involvement will depend on the age and ability of your child. We recommend that you read through any project in this book before it is undertaken.

EQUIPMENT

Each project has a list of everything you need to make it. You may already have many of these things at home, but check with an adult before taking anything. Use old wallpaper, brown parcel paper, or tracing paper to make the paper patterns that are to be pinned onto fabric. Use a tape measure or a ruler to make measurements. To make measurements on fabric, a fabric pencil is best, but depending on the fabric, a regular pencil or pen may work as well.

If you have a sewing basket at home, ask an adult if you can hunt through it for scissors, pins, needles, and thread. Pinking shears are good for cutting fabric since they stop material from fraying. A sewing machine is useful for stitching pieces of fabric together, but always ask an adult to help you use it. Store pencils, felt-tip pens, glue, paints, and brushes in a special box.

Get everything ready before you start, and don't forget to clean up afterward!

Read the instructions carefully before you begin.

BASIC TECHNIQUES

All the costumes featured in *My Costume Book* are easy to make. But before you start, we recommend that you learn some simple sewing techniques. On these pages you will find easy-to-follow instructions and step-by-step drawings for all the basic techniques we have used in the book. When you need to use a basic technique, the instructions for the costume you are making will tell you to refer to these pages.

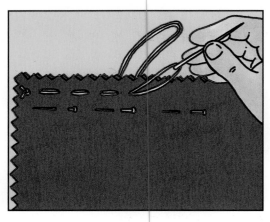

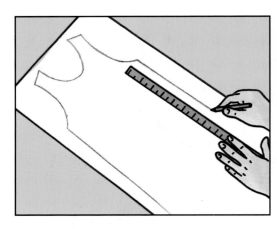

MAKING A PAPER PATTERN

To make a full-size paper pattern from a diagram at the back of the book, first lay out a large sheet of wallpaper, brown paper, or tracing paper on a flat surface. You will need a pencil, ruler, and a tape measure. Copy the diagram onto the paper, carefully following the measurements and starting with the longest straight lines. Before you cut the pattern out, check all the measurements again and make sure that the curved shapes look the same as on the diagram. Now cut out the paper pattern.

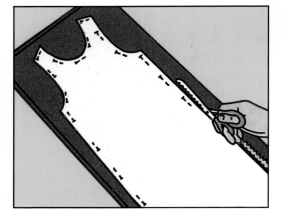

CUTTING OUT FABRIC

Check the instructions to see how many pieces of fabric you need to cut out. If you need to cut two pattern pieces that are the same, fold the fabric in half and pin the paper pattern onto both layers of fabric. Now cut around the paper pattern to give two identical fabric shapes. If you need just one pattern piece, pin the paper pattern onto a single layer of fabric and cut out. Always cut out fur fabric pattern pieces one at a time, making sure to cut through the back of the fabric.

RUNNING STITCH

A simple running stitch is used to sew pieces of fabric together. Unless the instructions say otherwise, place costume pieces right sides together. Pin the two pieces of fabric together, matching the raw edges.

Thread a needle with sewing thread, and make a knot at the end. Now push the needle through both layers of fabric, and pull the thread through to anchor the knot. Continue inserting the needle in and out of both layers of fabric, as shown, making the stitches about ¼ inch long and ⅝ inch in from the edges. Knot the thread at the end of the seam.

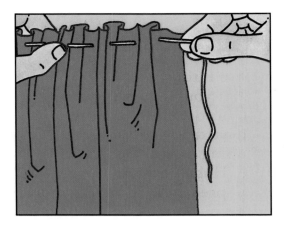

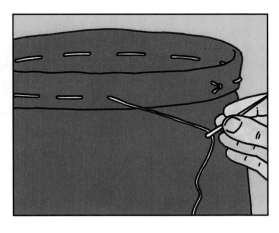

GATHERING FABRIC

1. Thread a needle with sewing thread, and make a knot at one end. Now sew a line of running stitches through the fabric, making the stitches about ½ inch long and ⅜ inch in from the edge. Do not make a knot when you have finished the stitching; leave the thread hanging. To gather up the fabric, gently pull the end of the thread and bunch up the fabric. If you are gathering up a long piece of fabric, divide the edge into quarters, and start and finish the gathers at these points.

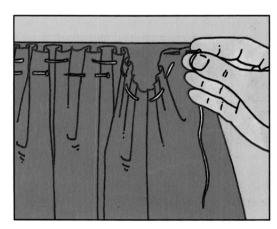

2. To attach the gathered piece of fabric to another piece of fabric, gently pull the gathers to fit and pin the frill in place. Stitch the two pieces of fabric together with small running stitches.

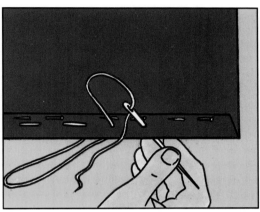

MAKING A HEM

Turn under ⅝ inch from the raw edge to the wrong side of the fabric. Pin the hem in position. Sew a neat line of running stitches through both layers of fabric. Now take out the pins.

MAKING A CASING

1. Turn under ¾ inch of fabric from the raw edge to the wrong side of the fabric. Sew a line of running stitches ⅝ inch from the folded edge to make a casing. If you are making the artist's smock or the mermaid's bikini top and tail, leave a small gap between the beginning and the end of your line of stitches.

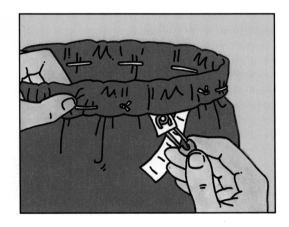

2. Attach a safety pin to one end of elastic, cord, or ribbon, and push the pin into the gap you left in the line of stitches. Feel for the pin through the fabric, and ease it through the casing, pushing back the fabric as you work. Pull the safety pin back out through the gap. If you are making the artist's smock or the mermaid's bikini top and tail, pin the ends of the elastic together. Try on the costume piece and adjust the elastic to fit. You may need to shorten the elastic if the costume piece is too big. Sew the ends of the elastic together.

PRESENT

For the ultimate gift—just present yourself! All you need for this costume is a large cardboard box and lots of wrapping paper. The crepe paper ribbon around the center of the present helps to disguise any seams in the gift wrap, and the large bow adds the finishing touch. Wear the box over a body stocking or a pair of tights with a T-shirt or leotard.

1 Cut the flaps off the bottom of the box. Cut out a 9-inch-diameter circle in the top of the box for your head to go through. Cut an oval about 6 inches wide and 9 inches high in each side of the box for your arms, 3¼ inches below the top edge.

YOU WILL NEED
A large cardboard box
Scissors; compass; ruler; pencil
2 large rolls of wrapping paper
Clear tape
Crepe paper; all-purpose glue
Colored card stock; felt-tip pen
31 inches of hat elastic
A body stocking (or a leotard or
  T-shirt and tights); a pair of socks

2 Cover the box with wrapping paper, using clear tape to hold it in place. Join the paper in the middle of the front, top, and back of the box, where the seams will be covered by crepe paper. Cut holes in the wrapping paper at the head and armholes, making them about ½ inch smaller than the box holes. Snip the wrapping paper to the edge of the box holes, as shown. Fold the snipped edges inside the box, and tape them in place.

3 Cut two long strips of crepe paper 7 inches wide, and glue them to the front and back of the box. Make a pleat at one end of each strip, as shown, and fold each end neatly inside the neck hole. Glue the ends in place inside the box. Glue the other ends of the crepe paper inside the bottom of the box.

4 Cut a large square of colored card stock for a gift tag. Cut a point at one end. Write your name on the tag with a felt-tip pen, and glue the tag to the box.

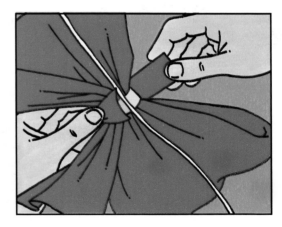

5 To make the bow headdress, cut a strip of crepe paper 32 inches long and 7 inches wide. Fold the ends to the center and glue them in place. Squeeze the middle of the strip, and hold it in place with tape. For the bow tails, cut a strip of crepe paper 20 inches long and 7 inches wide. Tape the midpoint of the strip to the middle of the bow. Next lay the hat elastic across the back of the bow. Wrap a narrow strip of crepe paper around the center of the bow, and secure the ends with glue.

PARISIAN ARTIST

Paint the town red—or yellow or blue—in this artistic costume. Use an old blouse or shirt for the artist's smock, and after shortening the sleeves, simply wear it back to front. The palette is made from a piece of thick card decorated with blobs of paint. The clever beard and jaunty beret will give you that distinguished look.

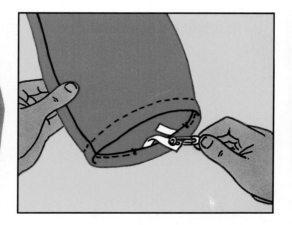

1 To make the artist's smock, cut the cuffs off the blouse sleeves. (If the blouse has a collar, you may want to cut it off as well.) Now make a casing at the bottom of each sleeve (see page 9). Using a safety pin, as described on page 9, thread each casing with a 7-inch length of elastic. Next fashion a bow from the black ribbon, and sew it into place at the back of the shirt. Wear the blouse back to front with the sleeves pushed up.

2 For the hat, cut out a circle of velvet with a 24-inch diameter. Sew large running stitches around the edge of the circle. Do not knot the thread when you are done, because you will be gathering this edge. Cut a length of webbing tape long enough to fit around your head plus 1¼ inches. Sew the short ends together.

SAFETY TIP: *Make sure an adult helps you when using wire.*

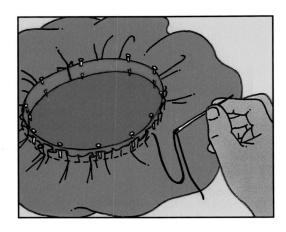

3 Gather the circle of green velvet to fit the tape by pulling the end of the thread. With the wrong side of the velvet on the outside, pin the tape to the inside of the gathered edge of the hat as shown. Stitch the gathers to the tape. Remove the pins, and turn the hat right side out.

4 To make the beard, ask an adult to help you bend the wire over one ear, under your mouth, and over your other ear. Remove the wire, and wrap the ends with masking tape so that it is comfortable to wear. Cut lots of 6½-inch lengths of gray yarn.

5 Fold the lengths of yarn in half. Knot the yarn over the wire by pulling the ends of the yarn through the loop as shown. To finish, cut a palette from thick beige card stock. Squeeze blobs of acrylic paint onto the card palette, and leave it to harden.

YOU WILL NEED
An adult's old blouse
Scissors; tape measure
Needle and thread; straight pins
Safety pin
A 7-inch length of elastic
A 36-inch length of wide black ribbon
A 28-by-36-inch piece of green velvet
Compass; fabric pencil
24 inches of webbing tape
A 16-inch length of thick wire
Masking tape
Gray yarn
Thick beige card stock
Acrylic paints
A pair of old pants
Sandals and paintbrush

FRIENDLY LION

You'll look like the king of the jungle in this striking outfit. The main item you need is a yellow body stocking, but you could substitute a yellow T-shirt or leotard and matching tights or leggings.

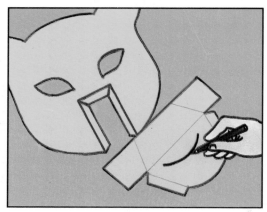

1 To make the mask, use a pencil and tracing paper to trace the face and muzzle patterns on pages 78 and 79. Lay the tracings facedown on yellow card stock and trace over the outlines. The patterns will appear on the card stock. Cut out along the solid lines. Draw the face details with a felt-tip pen.

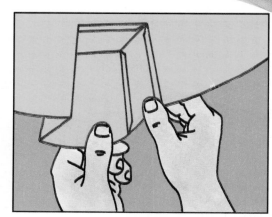

3 Fold the tabs on the face forward along the dotted lines. Glue the tabs to the inside of the muzzle as shown.

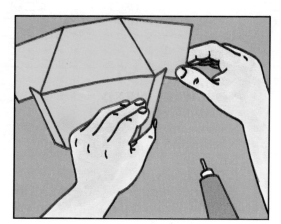

2 Fold the muzzle backward along the dotted lines. Erase any pencil marks. Fold the tabs backward, and glue them under the front edges of the muzzle.

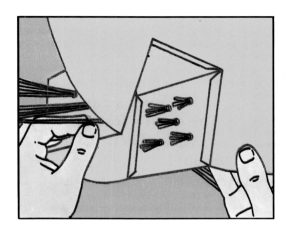

4 Using a pin, make small holes at the dots on the muzzle. Poke about five whiskers into each hole. Dab glue on the ends of the whiskers to keep them in place.

6 For the tail, cut a 28-by-4-inch strip of yellow fabric. Fold it in half (right sides together) and stitch the long edges together. Turn to the right side. Cut a 4½-inch square of fur fabric, and glue it around the end of the tail. Sew the tail to the back of the body stocking, leotard, or leggings.

YOU WILL NEED
Pencil; tracing paper
Yellow card stock; scissors
Felt-tip pen; all-purpose glue
A straight pin; black toy-making whiskers (from a craft store)
A 12-by-54-inch piece of golden fur fabric; measuring tape
Fabric pencil; needle and thread
20 inches of hat elastic
An 8-by-36-inch piece of yellow fabric
A yellow body stocking (or leotard and tights or T-shirt and leggings)
A pair of yellow socks

5 For the mane, cut a strip of fur fabric 54 inches by 4½ inches. Sew the short ends together on the wrong side of the fur. With a long length of double thread, sew running stitches along one long edge of the strip, and gather it into a circle (see Gathering Fabric, page 9). Glue the mane to the back of the mask. Make holes at the dots on the mask, and thread with elastic.

LITTLE DEVIL

This striking costume is perfect for a Halloween party. Make the cloak from deep red satin, and wear it over a dark-colored nightgown. The devil's fork is made from card stock, sticky-backed plastic, and an old broom handle painted red.

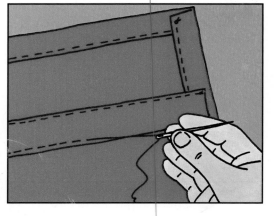

1 To make the cloak, cut a rectangle of red satin 51 inches long by 47 inches wide. Hem all the edges (see page 9).

2 To make the collar and bow, turn under 5/8 inch at each end of the bias binding, and stitch in place. Pin the bias binding to the wrong side of the cloak 3½ inches below one short edge. Stitch the bias binding to the cloak along the binding's long edges to make a casing. Attach a safety pin to one end of the narrow ribbon, and push it through the casing. Feel for the pin through the fabric, and ease it through the casing, pushing back the fabric. Pull the ribbon through the casing so that the ribbon ends are about the same length. Remove the safety pin. You will tie the ribbon in a bow to secure the cloak when you wear it.

YOU WILL NEED
1½ yards of 60-inch-wide satin
Measuring tape; fabric pencil
Scissors; needle and thread
Straight pins
1⅜ yards of red bias binding
2 yards of ½-inch-wide red ribbon
Safety pin; pencil; tracing paper
Red sticky-backed plastic; masking
    tape
Glue; 28 inches of hat elastic
Thick card stock; a broom handle
Red poster paint; paintbrush
1½ yards of 1¼-inch-wide
    red ribbon; a dark-colored
    nightgown

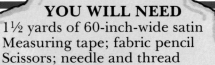

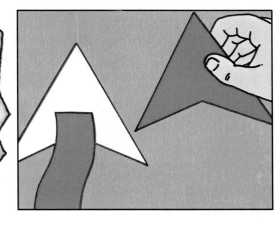

3 With a pencil and tracing paper, trace the horn pattern on page 79. Cut it out. Lay the pattern on a double layer of sticky-backed plastic, and hold it in place with masking tape. Cut out two horns. Do not remove the backing paper from the sticky-backed plastic. Overlap the straight edges, and glue them together. Make a hole on opposite sides of each horn near the bottom, and thread hat elastic through the holes. Knot the ends of the elastic so it fits under your chin.

4 To make the pitchfork, cover both sides of a piece of thick card stock with sticky-backed plastic. Cut out a fork shape using the photograph as a guide. Paint the cut edges red. Paint the broom handle red, and leave it to dry. Tape the broom handle to the back of the fork shape.

5 With a pencil and tracing paper, trace the tail end pattern on page 79. Follow the instructions in step 3 to cut two tail ends from sticky-backed plastic. Remove the backing paper from one tail end, and stick it onto one end of the wide ribbon. Stick the other tail end onto the first one, enclosing the ribbon. Use a safety pin to attach the tail to the back of the nightgown.

NOBLE KNIGHT

Transform yourself into a brave knight of old, ready to defend your kingdom from fire-breathing dragons. The tunic is easy to make from one large piece of fabric that you can decorate with your own coat of arms design. The trusty sword is cut from cardboard and decorated with silver paint and shapes cut from aluminum foil. Top your costume with a golden crown, and prepare to do battle.

YOU WILL NEED
A piece of fabric measuring 14 inches by 1¼ yards
Straight pins; fabric pencil
Ruler; scissors
Needle and thread
Colored felt
All-purpose glue
Corrugated cardboard
Sliver poster paint; paintbrush
Aluminum foil
Thin gold card stock
A gray long-sleeved T-shirt
Gray tights; a gray balaclava
Gray socks and gloves
A belt

1 To make the tunic, fold the fabric in half so that it measures 14 inches wide by 22½ inches long. Pin the folded edge in place. Along the folded edge, measure 4 inches in from the outside edge, and make a mark using the fabric pencil. Make a second mark a farther 6 inches along the folded edge. Measure 3 inches down from each point, and mark these measurements as well. With the pencil and ruler, draw lines connecting the four marks to make a rectangle, and cut it out, cutting through both thicknesses of fabric. Remove the pins.

2 Turn over all the rough edges, and neatly hem around the outside and the neck of the tunic with small, neat stitches. (You'll need to snip the neck corners to fold the rough edges in.) Cut out a shield shape from felt, and decorate it with a pattern cut from a different-colored piece of felt. Glue the pattern onto the shield, and then glue the shield onto the center of the front of the tunic.

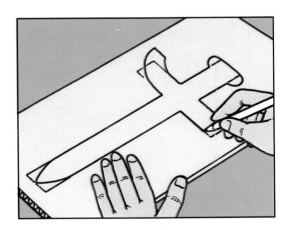

3 To make the sword, draw a large T shape on corrugated cardboard. Extend the long part of the T above the crossbar to make a basic sword shape. You might like to add curves to the end of the crossbar and a knob shape to the top of the handle as decoration. Follow the pictures here to guide you. Draw a point at the bottom of the sword. Cut out the shape you have drawn.

4 Paint the sword using silver poster paint, and leave it to dry. When the paint is dry, decorate the sword with shapes cut from aluminum foil. Make the decorative baubles and rivets by scrunching up small balls of foil. Glue the decorations onto the sword.

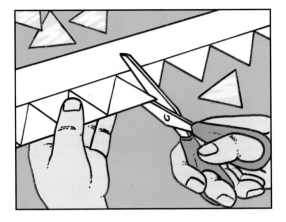

5 To make the crown, cut a strip of gold card stock measuring 2 inches wide and long enough to fit comfortably around your head. On the back of the card, draw a line running along the center of the strip. Draw a series of triangles from the top edge down to the center line to form a zigzag edge. Cut out the triangles. Wrap the crown around your head, and mark where the two edges cross. Glue the ends in place.

JACK-IN-THE-BOX

You can pop up at any masquerade party with this simple jack-in-the-box costume. If you don't have a body stocking, then a matching T-shirt and pants or leggings will do just as well. Draw a big spring on the body stocking or T-shirt with a fabric pen to make it look as if you've just sprung into action.

YOU WILL NEED
Ruler; pencil; scissors
Red and white card stock
All-purpose glue
Brass paper fasteners
2½ yards of green cord
Masking tape
Crepe paper; circle stickers
Needle and thread
A large cardboard box
Sticky-backed plastic; stickers
3¼ yards of wide polka-dot ribbon
Stapler; stuffed animals and dolls
Black fabric pen
A white body stocking (or
  a T-shirt and leggings)

1 To make the hat, cut a 24-by-5-inch strip of red card stock and two 24-by-1-inch strips of white card stock. Glue the white strips along each long edge of the red strip. Overlap the ends of the strip, and fasten them together by pushing brass paper fasteners through the white strips, as shown. Ask an adult to help you do this. Flatten the fastener prongs against the card stock.

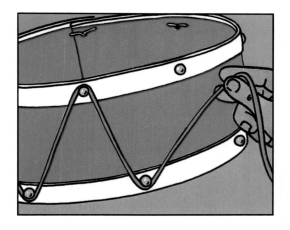

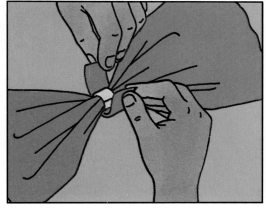

2 Push brass paper fasteners through the top white strip, about 3¾ inches apart. Then push more fasteners through the lower strip halfway between each top fastener. Thread cord up and down between the fasteners. Tie the ends of the cord together. Cover the backs of all the fasteners with masking tape.

3 To make the bow, cut an 11-by-6¼-inch rectangle of crepe paper. Squeeze tight at the center to make a bow, and fasten it with tape. Cover the tape with a narrow strip of crepe paper, and glue the ends together at the back of the bow. Decorate the bow with circle stickers. Sew the bow to the neck of the body stocking.

4 Cut the flaps off the top and bottom of the box. Cover the box with sticky-backed plastic. Then decorate the bow and box with stickers and shapes cut from more sticky-backed plastic.

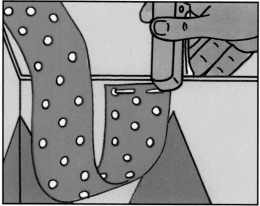

5 Cut the ribbon in half, and staple one end of each piece to the top of the box at the back. Try on the box, and pull the ribbons over your shoulders. Adjust the length of the ribbons, and staple the other ends to the front of the box. Use masking tape to attach a few toys to the inside of the box at the top.

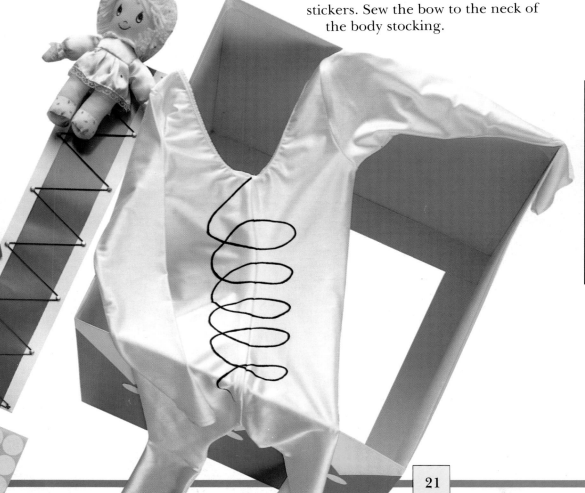

SOUTHERN BELLE

To make this elegant dress, we've actually used shiny green trash bags. You can find green bags in supermarkets and garden centers. Even the rose trims are made from plastic bags!

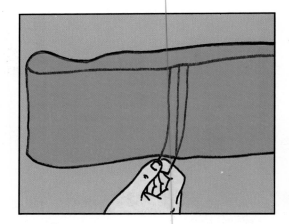

1 Cut away the neck of a T-shirt so that it is large enough to pull over your head without stretching. To make the ruffled collar, cut two 36-by-7¼-inch strips of plastic from a trash bag. Join the short sides edge-to-edge with clear tape.

2 Sew running stitches with a long, double length of thread along one long edge of the length of plastic, 1¼ inches below the upper edge. Pull the end of the thread to gather the plastic, and pin the ruffle to the neck of the T-shirt, pulling up the gathers to fit. (See Gathering Fabric, page 9.) Stitch the ruffle to the T-shirt, then remove the pins.

3 To make the skirt, cut two 31-by-20-inch rectangles of plastic from trash bags. Join the short sides edge-to-edge with clear tape to make one long strip. (Continued on the next page).

YOU WILL NEED
A T-shirt
Scissors; tape measure; pencil
Large trash bags
Clear tape
Needle and thread; straight pins
Red sticky-backed plastic
Double-sided tape
Stick-on Velcro; child's umbrella
31 inches of ribbon
Colored plastic shopping bags
Stapler
A pair of gloves
2 hair combs

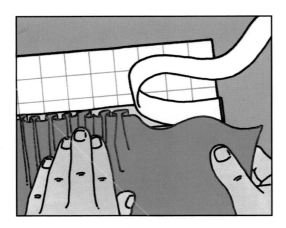

4 For the waistband, cut a strip of sticky-backed plastic 2 inches wide and long enough to fit around your waist plus 2 inches. Stick a strip of double-sided tape along one long edge of the backing paper. Gradually peel the backing paper off the double-sided tape, and stick one long edge of the skirt onto the waistband, gathering the plastic to fit.

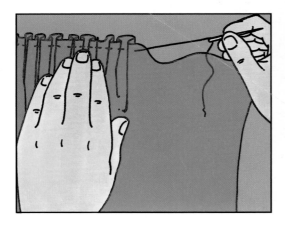

5 To make the skirt ruffles, cut three 31-by-17-inch rectangles of plastic from trash bags. Join the short sides edge-to-edge with clear tape to make one long strip. Sew running stitches along one long edge of the strip, 1¼ inches below the upper edge, and gather the plastic, as in step 2.

6 Pin the ruffle onto the lower edge of the skirt, gently pulling up the gathers to fit. Sew the ruffle in place, then remove the pins. Join most of the back seam of the skirt and ruffle with clear tape. Attach stick-on Velcro pads to the ends of the waistband. When you put the skirt on, have a friend help you finish taping the back seam.

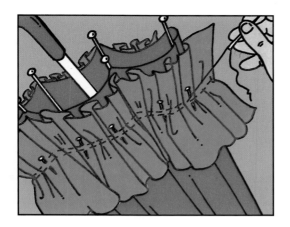

7 To make the ruffle for the parasol, cut three 40-by-5-inch strips of plastic from trash bags. Join the short sides together with clear tape to make one long strip. Sew running stitches along the center of the strip, and gather the plastic as before. Pin the ruffle to the umbrella, gently pulling up the gathers to fit. Sew the ruffle in place. Tie the ribbon in a bow around the handle.

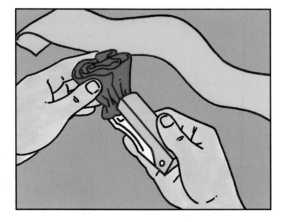

8 To make the roses, cut 19-by-5-inch strips for large roses and 14-by-3¼-inch strips for small roses from colored plastic bags. Fold the strips in half lengthwise. Starting at one end, roll the strips, making little pleats on the lower long edges. Staple the lower edges together at intervals. Sew a few small roses to the gloves, parasol, and hair combs. Sew large and small roses to the T-shirt and skirt.

STRONGMAN

If you wear this super strongman outfit to a Halloween party, we can guarantee you'll be the main attraction. Use face paints to add a bushy moustache and some colorful tattoos, and you're ready to go!

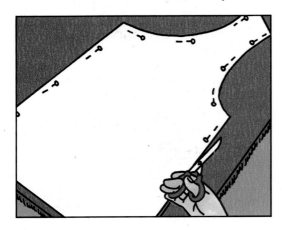

1 To make the tunic, you will first need to make a full-size paper pattern following the diagram on page 80. To find out how to do this and how to cut out fabric, read the instructions on page 8. Now cut out two fur fabric tunic shapes. Then cut a ragged edge along the bottom of both.

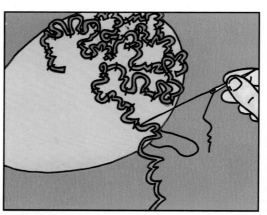

3 For the hairy chest, cut out a large oval of stockinette. Arrange strands of yarn on top, and stitch them in place. Stick the hairy chest to your chest with double-sided tape.

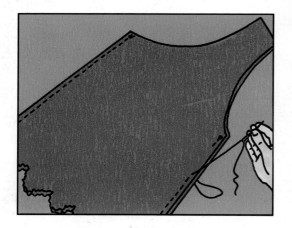

2 Pin the tunic shapes right sides together. Stitch them together along the side seams and across the shoulder using running stitches (see page 8).

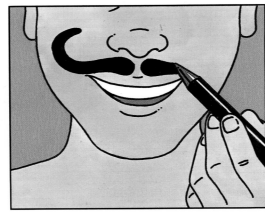

YOU WILL NEED
Paper; pencil; ruler; scissors
A 40-by-54-inch piece of fur
  fabric; straight pins
Needle and thread
Stockinette; brown yarn
Double-sided tape
Length of broom handle (or 1-inch
  dowel); 2 rubber balls
All-purpose glue; black poster
  paint; paintbrush; face paints

4 To make the dumbbell, ask an adult to cut an 18-inch length of broom handle. Glue a rubber ball to each end of the broom handle. Paint the balls and the broom handle black. Leave the dumbbell to dry.

5 To complete your outfit, use face paints to give yourself a bushy moustache and to draw some colorful tattoos on your arms.

SCARECROW

This colorful outfit is really easy to put together, and it looks great. You will need some old clothes and a pair of rubber boots. If you don't have these at home, you can buy them cheaply from a local secondhand clothes store.

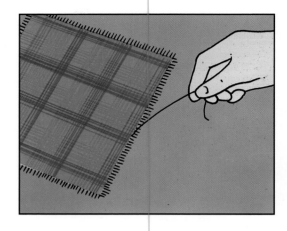

2 To make the bandana, cut out a square of fabric. Fray the edges by pulling out three or four threads from all four sides.

1 Cut a ragged edge around the sleeves of the old shirt and around the legs of the old pair of pants. Cut out patches of colorful fabric, and sew them to the shirt and pants. Glue pieces of straw to the bottom of the shirtsleeves.

YOU WILL NEED
An old shirt; an old pair of pants; scissors
Scraps of fabric
Needle and thread
Straw; all-purpose glue
1-inch-wide elastic
A pair of rubber boots; an old hat
Pencil; tracing paper
Orange card stock; 20 inches of hat elastic

3 Cut two lengths of wide elastic long enough to wrap around the tops of the rubber boots. Sew pieces of straw to the elastic. Overlap the ends of the elastic, and sew them together. Slip the elastic over the tops of the boots.

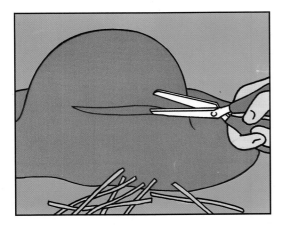

4 Cut a slit across the crown, or top section, of the hat. Glue straw inside the hat, and pull it through the slit. Glue more straw inside the brim of the hat so that it hangs down.

5 To make the nose, use a pencil and tracing paper to trace the pattern on page 80. Turn your tracing over, and lay it on the orange card stock. Trace over the pencil lines to transfer the nose shape onto the card stock. Cut out the nose, overlap the straight edges, and glue them together. Make a hole at each side of the nose. Thread elastic through the holes, and knot the ends inside the nose.

RAG DOLL

Look for some bright polka-dot fabric to make this colorful rag doll dress. If you have a sewing machine at home, ask an adult to help you use it to sew up the side seams instead of sewing them by hand. An old pair of tights and some yarn are used to make the chunky braids. Use face paints to give yourself rosy cheeks and long eyelashes.

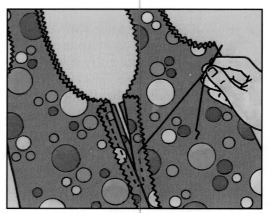

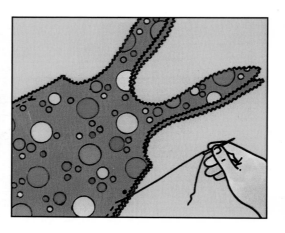

2 Turn back the raw edges at the top of the side seams, and sew the edges down. Cut the narrow ribbon into quarters, and sew one piece to the top of each underarm edge. Turn the dress right side out, and sew lace around the bottom edge.

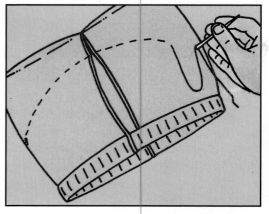

1 To make the dress, you will first need to make a full-size paper pattern following the diagram on page 81. To find out how to do this and how to cut out fabric, read the instructions on page 8. Now use pinking shears to cut out two dress pieces from polka-dot fabric. Pin the pieces right sides together, and sew along the side seams using running stitches (see page 8). Leave a 4-inch gap below each armhole. Remove the pins.

SAFETY TIP: *Make sure an adult helps you when using wire.*

3 For the wig, cut the legs off of a pair of tights. Match the front and back seams, and stitch across the cut edge in a curve to make a skullcap. Turn the cap right side out.

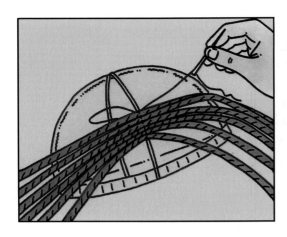

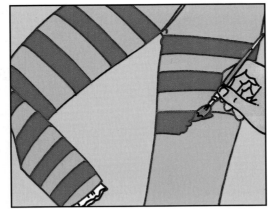

YOU WILL NEED

Paper; pencil; ruler; scissors

2⅜ yards of 36-inch-wide polka-dot fabric; straight pins

Pinking shears; needle and thread

1⅜ yards of narrow yellow ribbon

1⅝ yards of lace edging

An old pair of tights

Brown yarn; rubber bands

Two 8-inch lengths of thick wire

Masking tape

1¾ yards each of wide green and blue ribbon; a pair of yellow leggings

Red fabric paints; paintbrush

Plastic bags; all-purpose glue

A pair of shoes; face paints

4 Cut lots of 40-inch lengths of yarn. Sew the middle of each length of yarn to the seam of the skullcap. Try the wig on, and gather the "hair" into a bunch at each side of your face. Tie a length of yarn around the top of each bunch. Take the wig off, and braid the bunches. Fasten the ends together with a rubber band.

6 Before you paint stripes on the leggings, push a plastic bag down into the legs so that the fabric paint does not seep through to the other side. Paint stripes on one side of the leggings with fabric paint. Leave them to dry, then paint the other side. Cut the wide blue ribbon in half, and tie each length into a bow. Glue or tie the bows to your shoes.

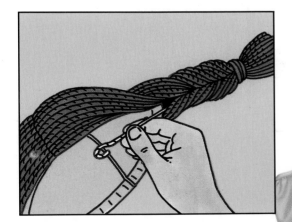

5 Wrap the ends of the wire with masking tape. Bend one end of each piece of wire into a loop. Starting at the top of the braid, push the other end of the wire down through the braid. Sew the looped end of each wire to the skullcap. Bend the wire to give the braids a curled-up shape. Cut the wide green ribbon in half, and tie a bow around the bottom of each braid to hide the rubber band.

TV SET

This is the perfect costume for all budding TV stars. A large cardboard box is all that is needed for the case. Keep the background plain and wear a colorful T-shirt to make the picture really stand out. Make a wire TV antenna, and top the box with a plant or a bowl of artificial fruit.

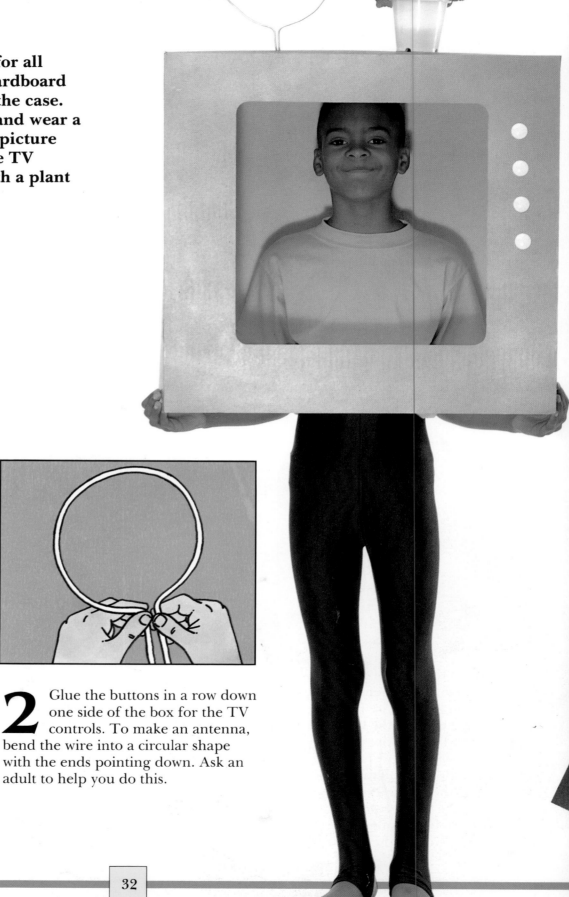

1 Cut the flaps from the bottom of the box. Now cut a square out of one side of the box for the television screen. Paint the box gray, and leave it to dry. Glue a square of blue card stock to the inside back of the box for the background.

2 Glue the buttons in a row down one side of the box for the TV controls. To make an antenna, bend the wire into a circular shape with the ends pointing down. Ask an adult to help you do this.

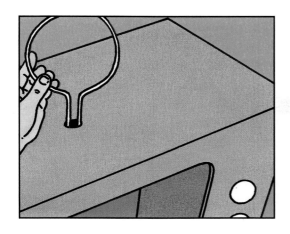

3 Pierce a hole in the top of the box with a knitting needle. You may need some help with this. Push the ends of the antenna into the hole. Bend the ends of the wire flat against the top of the box on the inside. Tape the wire in place.

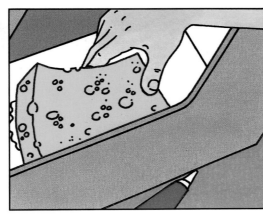

4 To make the TV set comfortable to wear, glue a square of foam to the inside top of the box. Position the foam in the center so it will rest on your head. To finish, glue an artificial plant pot to the top of the television.

YOU WILL NEED
Scissors
A large cardboard box
Gray poster paint; paintbrush
Blue card stock; all-purpose glue
4 flat buttons
Thick wire
Knitting needle
Masking tape
A 6-inch square of thick foam or
   sponge
Artificial potted plant
A T-shirt; leggings or pants

FLOWER FAIRIES

Flower fairies come in every color imaginable. Use pink or mauve fabric to make the dress as shown here, or choose a color that matches a leotard you already have. You may want to ask an adult to help you make this costume, since it is a little more difficult than most of the others featured in the book. If you have a sewing machine at home, ask an adult to help you use it to sew the dress.

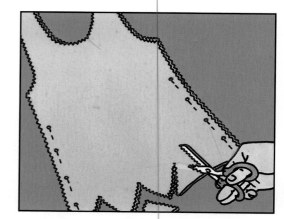

1 To make the dress, you will first need to make a full-size paper pattern following the diagram on page 81. To find out how to do this and how to cut out fabric, read the instructions on page 8. Now use pinking shears to cut out four dress pieces from organza. Pin the dress pieces together in pairs, and cut a scalloped edge to look like petals along the bottom of each pair.

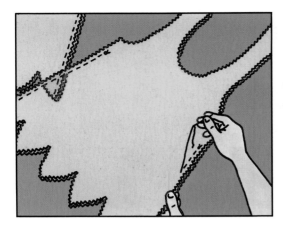

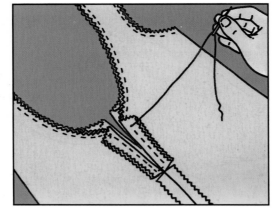

2 Now sew each pair of dress pieces together along the side seams, using running stitches (see page 8). Leave a 4-inch gap below each armhole as shown. Snip the fabric to the seam at the start of the gap.

3 Slip one dress inside the other, matching the armholes and the gaps at the top of the side seams. Stitch the armholes, neck edges, and shoulder straps together close to the raw edges, or fold the fabric over and stitch in place. Fold over the double layer of fabric at the top of the side seams, and sew in place as shown.

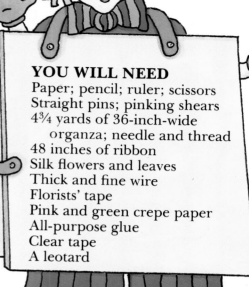

YOU WILL NEED
Paper; pencil; ruler; scissors
Straight pins; pinking shears
4¾ yards of 36-inch-wide
  organza; needle and thread
48 inches of ribbon
Silk flowers and leaves
Thick and fine wire
Florists' tape
Pink and green crepe paper
All-purpose glue
Clear tape
A leotard

(Continued on the next page)

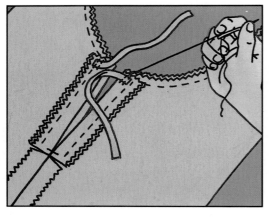

4 Cut the ribbon into four equal lengths, and sew one piece to the top of each underarm edge, as shown. Turn the dress right side out. When you wear the dress, tie the pieces of ribbon together in a bow under each arm and tie the shoulder straps together as well.

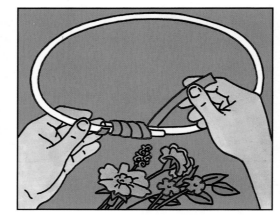

6 To make the headdress, ask an adult to cut a length of thick wire large enough to wrap around your head. Overlap the ends of the wire, and fasten them with florists' tape. Attach small silk flowers to the headdress with florists' tape. Make a bracelet and ankle bracelet in the same way.

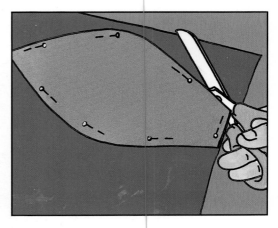

7 For the petal hat, make a full-size paper pattern following the petal diagram on page 80. Pin the pattern onto pink crepe paper, and cut out one petal. Repeat to cut out nine more petals.

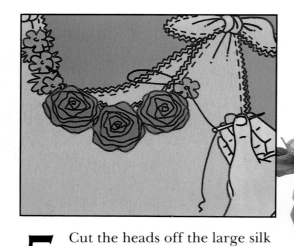

5 Cut the heads off the large silk flowers, and sew them around the neck of the dress at the front. Sew some smaller flowers between the large flowers.

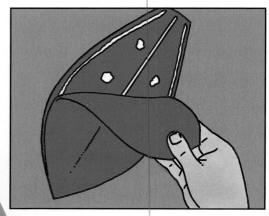

8 Now cut five lengths of fine wire 10 inches long. Spread glue on five of the petals, and lay a length of wire down the center of each one. Press one of the remaining petals to each glued petal, enclosing the wire.

SAFETY TIP: *Make sure an adult helps you when using wire.*

9 Join the petals together edge-to-edge at the top, and stick strips of tape across the seams as shown. Bind the points of the petals upward.

10 Squeeze the tops of the petals together to make a hat shape, and hold the hat top in place with clear tape. Glue silk leaves around the top of the hat. Glue a narrow strip of green crepe paper around the bound top.

PIRATE

All you need is a vest to turn a striped T-shirt and polka-dotted scarf into an authentic pirate outfit. Add a black eye patch, a moustache, and an earring to complete the costume. You'll also need to arm yourself with a saber and telescope to guard against enemy ships. Look for these in toy stores (or make your own!).

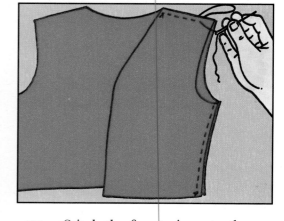

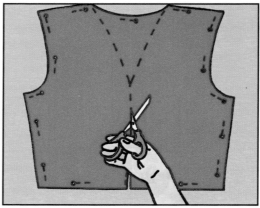

1 To make the vest, you will first need to make a full-size paper pattern following the diagram on page 82. To find out how to do this and how to cut out fabric, read the instructions on page 8. Now cut out two vest shapes from felt along the solid lines shown on the pattern. Pin the paper pattern back onto one of the shapes, and cut the felt along the broken lines to make two front pieces.

2 Stitch the front pieces to the back along the side seams and shoulder seams, as shown. Turn the vest right side out, and sew the buttons to the front edges.

YOU WILL NEED

Paper; pencil; ruler; scissors
A 16-by-36-inch piece of felt
Straight pins; needle and thread
6 gold buttons
Black card stock
28 inches of hat elastic
Double-sided tape
Polka-dotted headscarf
Brass curtain ring
Clip-on earring back
A pair of old pants; a black belt
A striped T-shirt

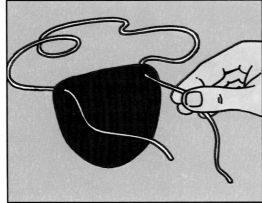

3 Cut an eye patch from black card stock. Make a hole at each side and thread with elastic. Knot the ends of the elastic together.

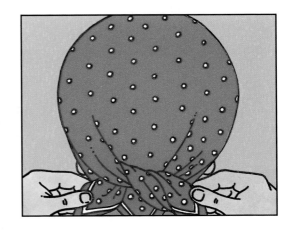

5 Fold the scarf in half diagonally. Place it across your forehead, and knot the ends together at the back, as shown. To make an earring, attach a brass curtain ring to a clip-on earring back. To finish your costume, cut a ragged edge along the bottom of the pant legs and wear them with a black belt.

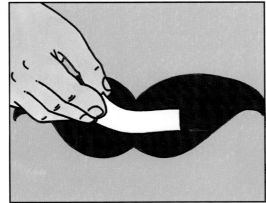

4 Cut a moustache from black card stock. Stick a length of double-sided tape on the back, and stick the moustache just above your upper lip.

ICE MAIDEN

Stay cool in this beautiful icy costume that sparkles with every move. A white leotard or bathing suit forms the base for the outfit, which is decorated with an eye-catching iridescent skirt and shoulder frill. Add a pair of silver ballet slippers, a wand, and a crown to complete the sophisticated look.

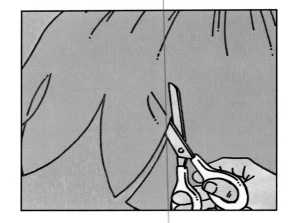

1 Cut a strip of iridescent cellophane 70 inches long by 12 inches wide for the skirt and a second strip 70 inches long by 5 inches wide for the shoulder frill. Join the pieces of cellophane with tape if necessary. Cut points along one long edge of the skirt and the frill.

YOU WILL NEED
Iridescent cellophane
Tape measure; fabric pencil
Scissors; clear tape
Silver sticky-backed plastic
Double-sided tape
Stick-on Velcro
Card stock; all-purpose glue
Tracing paper; pencil
A 15-inch length of ¼-inch dowel
Silver acrylic paint; paintbrush
Narrow gift-wrap ribbon
Plastic gemstones
40 inches of fine silver elastic
A white leotard
Silver or white ballet slippers

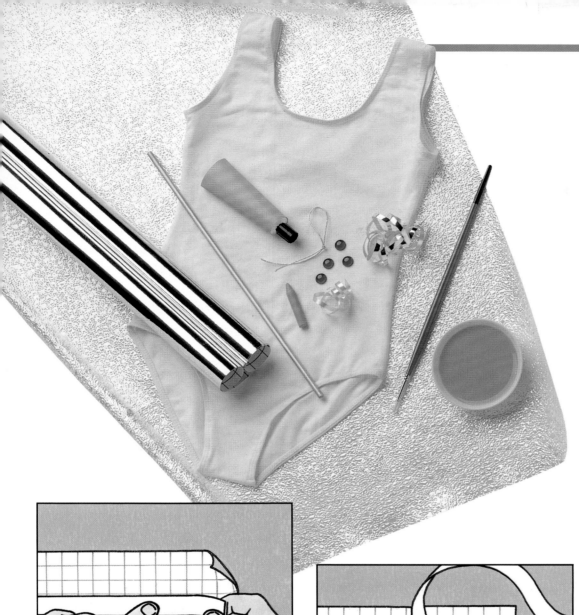

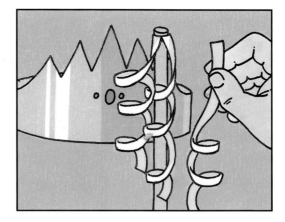

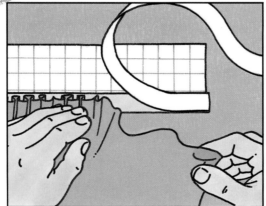

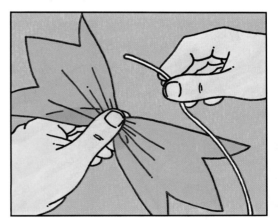

4 To make the crown, cover a piece of card stock with silver sticky-backed plastic. Trace the pattern on page 82, and extend the sides so the crown will fit around your head. Tape the pattern to the silver-covered card stock. Cut out the crown, and glue the ends together. To make the wand, cut a star from silver card stock. Paint the dowel silver, and glue gift-wrap ribbon to the top. Glue the star to the stick. Glue gemstones to the crown, star, and waistband.

2 For the waistband, cut a strip of silver sticky-backed plastic 2 inches wide and long enough to fit around your waist plus 2 inches. Cut another strip 31 inches long by ¾ inch wide for the shoulder band. Stick double-sided tape along one long edge of the backing paper on the waistband and the shoulder band. Do not remove the backing paper from the sticky-backed plastic.

3 To make the skirt, gradually peel the backing paper off the double-sided tape on the waistband, and stick the long, straight edge of the skirt to the tape. Gather up the skirt to fit. Join the frill to the shoulder band in the same way. Stick Velcro pads on the ends of the waistband and the shoulder band for fastening.

5 For the ankle and wrist decorations, cut four 7-by-7-inch squares of iridescent cellophane. Cut points along two opposite edges of each square. Cut the elastic into quarters, and tie each piece tightly around the center of each square. Knot the elastic around your wrists and ankles. To finish, tape gift-wrap ribbon to one shoulder of the leotard.

SPACE HEROES

A leotard and a pair of leggings are the main ingredients for this space-age outfit. The collar, waistband, and gauntlets are all made from silver sticky-backed plastic. A pair of rubber boots painted silver and decorated with shiny stars will complete the look.

1 To make the collar, cut an 18-by-16-inch rectangle of silver sticky-backed plastic. The 18-inch sides form the front and back of the collar. In the middle of the collar, cut a rectangle big enough to fit your neck through. Now cut from the center back of the collar to the edge of the neck square. Stick Velcro pads onto the edges of the collar for fastening.

2 Cut a decorative edge along the sides of the collar, leaving a long tab of sticky-backed plastic at the top and bottom of each side. Stick Velcro pads on these tabs; when you put on the collar, fasten the tabs together under your arms. Do not remove the backing paper from the sticky-backed plastic. Cut a star from colored sticky-backed plastic, and stick it to the front of the collar.

4 For the belt, cut a strip of silver sticky-backed plastic 2 inches wide and long enough to fit around your waist plus 2 inches. Do not remove the backing paper from the sticky-backed plastic. Stick Velcro pads on the ends of the belt for fastening. Paint the boots silver. Decorate each boot with a star cut from colored sticky-backed plastic.

5 To make the headdress, stick silver sticky-backed plastic to card stock, and cut out a star shape. Attach the star to the middle of the length of narrow ribbon with double-sided tape. Tie the ribbon around your head with the star at the front.

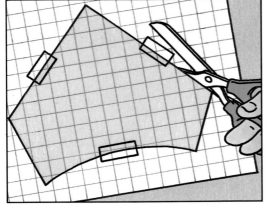

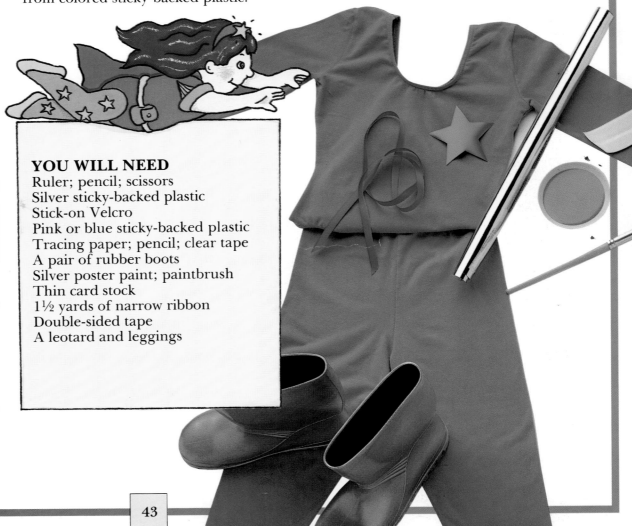

3 To make the gauntlets, trace and cut out the pattern on page 83. Lay the pattern on a double layer of silver sticky-backed plastic, and hold it in place with clear tape. Cut out two gauntlets. Decorate each gauntlet with a star cut from colored sticky-backed plastic. Stick Velcro pads on the edges of the gauntlets for fastening around your wrists.

YOU WILL NEED
Ruler; pencil; scissors
Silver sticky-backed plastic
Stick-on Velcro
Pink or blue sticky-backed plastic
Tracing paper; pencil; clear tape
A pair of rubber boots
Silver poster paint; paintbrush
Thin card stock
1½ yards of narrow ribbon
Double-sided tape
A leotard and leggings

BLACK CAT

A black body stocking or a leotard or a T-shirt and tights are the main essentials for this feline outfit. Added to this are a fluffy white tummy, soft ears, a slinky tail, and paws. The nose is made from a single section of an egg carton. A toy mouse to play with completes the look.

2 For the nose, cut a section from the egg carton. Paint the section white, and leave it to dry. Draw on a muzzle with a red felt-tip pen. Make three small holes at each side of the nose, and push about five whiskers into each hole. Dab glue on the ends of the whiskers to keep them in place. Make two more holes at each side of the nose close to the edge, and thread hat elastic through them. Knot the elastic inside the nose.

1 To make the ears, trace and cut out the ear pattern on page 83. Pin the pattern onto a double layer of pink felt, and cut out two ear shapes. Remove the pattern, and pin it to the back of the black fur fabric. Cut out one ear, and then repeat to cut out a second ear. Stitch a felt ear to the wrong side of a fur ear. Do not stitch across the bottom edge. Turn the ears right side out, and pin them to the headband. Sew them in place, then remove the pins.

SAFETY TIP: *Make sure an adult helps you when using wire.*

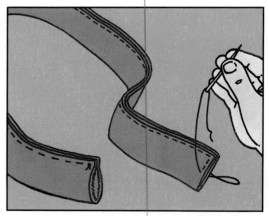

3 Cut out a large oval of white fur fabric for the tummy, and sew it to the body stocking. For the tail, cut a strip of black fur fabric 28 inches long by 5 inches wide. Fold it in half lengthwise, wrong side out. Stitch along the long edge and across one end. Turn the tail right side out.

44

4 Wrap the ends of the wire with masking tape, and then bend each end into a loop. Ask an adult to help you do this. Slip the tail over the wire, and sew the end of the wire and the open end of the tail to the back of the body stocking. Bend the tail into a draping curve shape. To finish, cut out pink felt paw pads, and glue them to the palms of the gloves.

YOU WILL NEED
Tracing paper; pencil
Pink felt; straight pins; scissors
A 28-square-inch piece of black fur fabric; needle and thread
A black velvet headband
Cardboard egg carton
White poster paint; paintbrush
Red felt-tip pen
Black toy-making whiskers (from a craft store); all-purpose glue
20 inches of hat elastic
A 16-square-inch piece of white fur fabric
A black body stocking (or a leotard or T-shirt and tights); black gloves
28 inches of thick wire; masking tape

GRANDFATHER CLOCK

You'll be sure to get to the party on time in this unusual Grandfather Clock costume. The brown moiré fabric has a wood-effect pattern, which is perfect for the clock case. If you have a sewing machine at home, ask an adult to help you use it to sew the side seams together instead of sewing them by hand. To complete the costume, glue toy mice to the tunic and the hat.

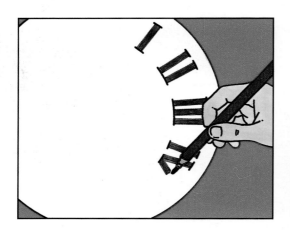

1 Using a pencil and tracing paper, trace the clock pattern on page 84. Cut out the circle. Do not cut out the hands. Pin the pattern onto the square of white fabric, and cut out the shape. Use a fabric pen to copy the Roman numerals shown on the pattern onto the clock face. Leave it to dry.

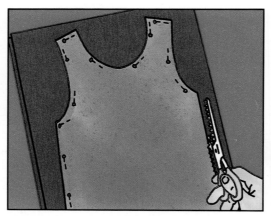

2 To make the tunic, you will first need to make a full-size paper pattern following the diagram on page 86. To find out how to do this and how to cut out fabric, read the instructions on page 8. Now use pinking shears to cut out two tunic pieces from the moiré fabric.

3 Glue the clock face to the front of one of the tunic pieces 4 inches below the neck edge. Glue or sew gold cord around the edge of the clock face.

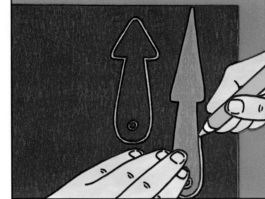

4 Cut out the tracings of the clock hands. Position them on the black card stock, and trace around the shapes with a colored pencil. Cut out the hands. Use scissor points to make a hole at the dots on the hands and through the center of the clock face. Ask an adult to help you.

YOU WILL NEED
Tracing paper; pencil; scissors
Straight pins; black fabric pen
12 square inches of white fabric
3½ yards of 36-inch-wide brown moiré fabric; ruler
Pinking shears; all-purpose glue
1 yard of gold cord
Black, brown, and gold card stock
Colored pencil
A brass paper fastener; masking tape
Needle and thread
A 24-inch length of brown ribbon
Toy mice

(Continued on the next page)

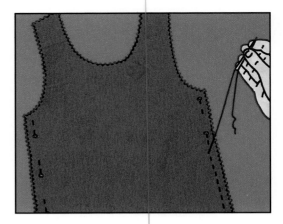

6 Pin the two tunic pieces right sides together. Stitch them together along the side seams, using running stitches (see page 8).

5 Push a brass paper fastener through the holes on the hands and then through the clock face. Open out the prongs on the underside of the clock, and flatten them against the fabric. Stick some masking tape over the prongs to hold them in place.

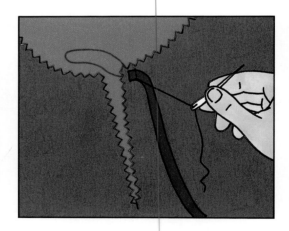

7 Use pinking shears to cut a slit about 4 inches long from the center of the neck edge of the back tunic piece. Cut the ribbon in half, and sew one end of each length to each side of the slit. You'll tie the ribbon in a bow when you wear the costume. Turn the tunic right side out.

9 Now lay the small molding pattern on gold card stock, and trace around it. Cut out the shape, and lay it back on the card stock. Trace around the shape, and cut out a second molding. Glue one of the moldings to the brown moiré clock top. Cut a strip of brown card stock 24 inches long by 1 inch wide. Glue the ends together. Then glue the clock top to the front of the strip.

8 To make the hat, trace and cut out the patterns for the clock top and the small molding on page 85. Lay the clock top pattern on brown card stock, and trace around the shape with a pencil. Cut out the shape. Glue the brown card stock clock top onto a piece of moiré fabric. Trim away the fabric from around the edges of the card stock.

10 Glue the second small gold molding to the tunic just below the clock. Trace and cut out the pattern of the large molding on page 85. Lay the pattern on gold card stock, and trace around it. Cut out the shape, and glue it to the bottom of the tunic. To finish, glue toy mice to the tunic and the hat.

WICKED WITCH

From the ugly green nose to the long witchy fingernails, this is the perfect outfit for Halloween! Make or borrow a twig broom and decorate your costume with plastic creepy-crawlies bought from a toy shop to add the finishing touches. Choose face paints in green and black to make sure you look suitably bewitching.

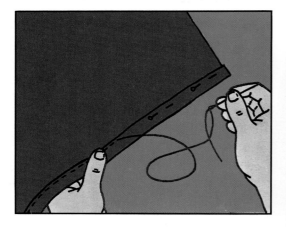

1 To make the cloak, cut a 47-by-47-inch piece of purple fabric. Make a hem on two opposite edges (see page 9).

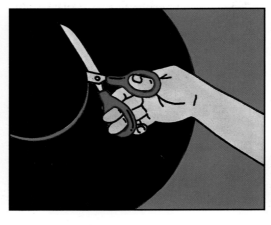

3 To make the hat brim, cut out a circle with a 15-inch diameter from black felt. Cut a hole with a 5½-inch diameter in the center of the hat brim.

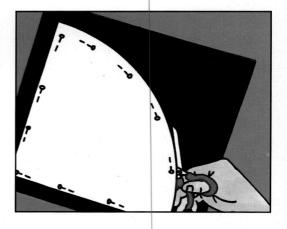

4 For the cone of the hat, draw a full-size paper pattern, following the diagram on page 86. Cut out the pattern, and pin it to black felt. Cut out the cone shape, and remove the pattern. Spray the cone and the brim with starch, and ask an adult to help you iron them.

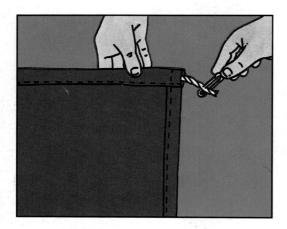

2 Make a casing on one raw edge of the cloak (see page 9). Use a safety pin to thread the casing with cord. This is the top edge of the cloak. Cut a jagged edge along the bottom of the cloak and nightgown.

SAFETY TIP: *Make sure an adult helps you when using an iron.*

5 Fold the cone in half and sew the straight edges together. Pin the cone into the hole in the brim, and stitch in place as shown. Cut lots of lengths of green yarn, and glue them inside the hat for hair. Stuff tissue paper into the top of the cone to make it stand upright.

6 Trace the nose pattern on page 86. Lay the tracing facedown on green card stock. Trace over the pencil lines to transfer the shape to the card stock. Cut it out. Fold the nose backward along the fold line. Glue the tab under the opposite side. Make holes at either side of the nose, and thread elastic through them. Knot the elastic inside the nose. Cut long fingernails from green card stock, and stick them onto your own nails with double-sided tape.

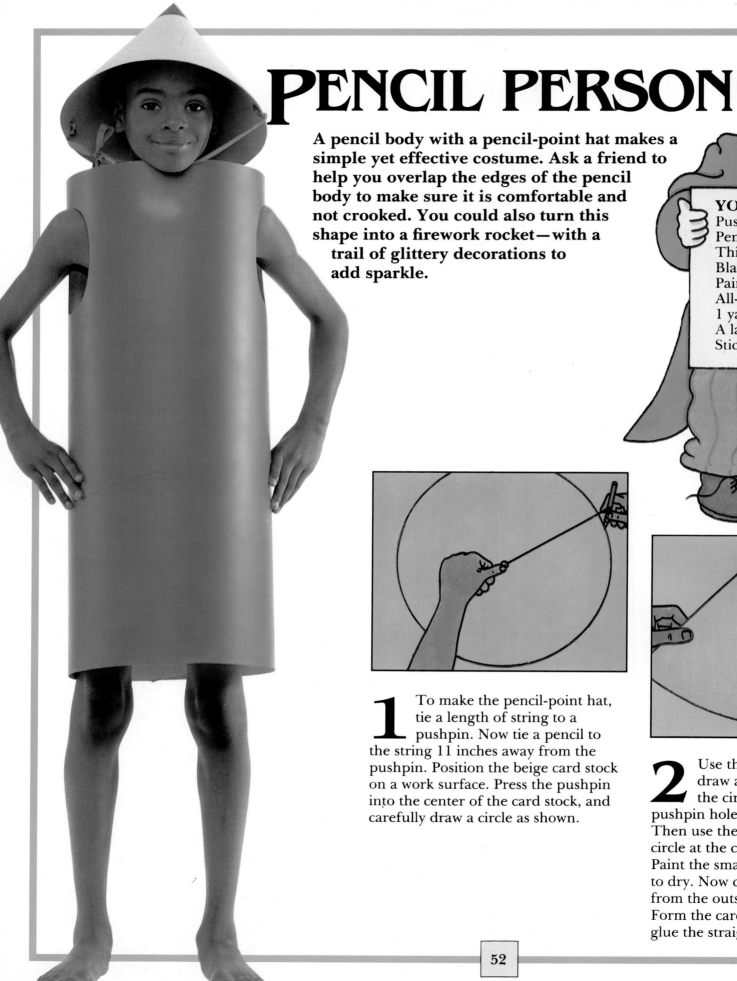

PENCIL PERSON

A pencil body with a pencil-point hat makes a simple yet effective costume. Ask a friend to help you overlap the edges of the pencil body to make sure it is comfortable and not crooked. You could also turn this shape into a firework rocket—with a trail of glittery decorations to add sparkle.

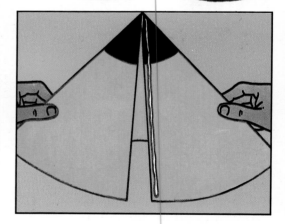

YOU WILL NEED
Pushpin; string; ruler
Pencil; scissors; compass
Thin beige card stock
Black and blue poster paints
Paintbrush
All-purpose glue; hole punch
1 yard of blue ribbon
A large piece of card stock
Stick-on Velcro

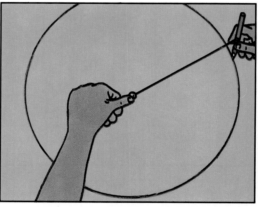

1 To make the pencil-point hat, tie a length of string to a pushpin. Now tie a pencil to the string 11 inches away from the pushpin. Position the beige card stock on a work surface. Press the pushpin into the center of the card stock, and carefully draw a circle as shown.

2 Use the ruler and pencil to draw a line from the center of the circle (marked by the pushpin hole) to the outside edge. Then use the compass to draw a small circle at the center of the larger circle. Paint the small circle black and leave it to dry. Now cut along the penciled line from the outside edge to the center. Form the card stock into a cone, and glue the straight edges together.

3 Punch a hole on either side of the hat. Cut the length of ribbon in half, and poke each end through the holes. Knot the ends of the ribbon inside the hat.

4 To make the body shape, cut a length of card stock large enough to wrap around your body. Cut out ovals for armholes at each side of the card stock 2 inches below the upper edge. Paint the card stock blue, and leave it to dry. Try on the costume, and ask a friend to help you overlap the edges at the back and fasten them with stick-on Velcro.

MYTHICAL MERMAID

Choose green or blue metallic fabric to make this exotic mermaid costume with shells collected from the beach, or buy gold-colored shells from a craft or department store. Sew sequins on your leggings to give the effect of shimmering fish scales. The tail is cleverly elasticized at the knees to allow you to walk around!

1 To make the wig, cut the legs off the pair of tights. Matching the seams together, stitch across the cut edge in a curve to make a skullcap. Turn the cap right side out.

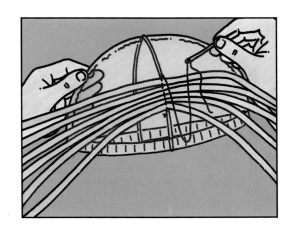

2 Cut lots of 43-inch lengths of yarn. Fold the lengths of yarn in half. Sew each piece of yarn to the center seam of the skullcap. Do this until the skullcap is completely covered.

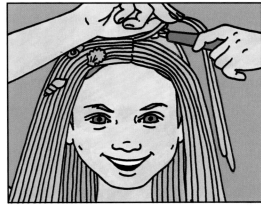

3 Put on the shower cap or bathing cap, then try on the wig (the cap will protect your hair from the glue). Lift up sections of the yarn close to the stitching, and glue them to the skullcap. Glue shells to the wig while you are wearing it. Ask an adult to help you do this. (Continued on the next page)

YOU WILL NEED
A pair of old tights
Scissors
Needle and thread
Yarn
Old shower or bathing cap
All-purpose glue; shells
1¼ yard of 60-inch-wide metallic fabric
2½ yards of elastic; safety pin

Fine ribbon
Paper; pencil
Pinking shears
Large sequins
A pair of blue leggings
Plastic beaded necklaces

4 To make the bikini top, cut a strip of metallic fabric 6 inches by 32 inches long. Sew the ends together.

5 Make a casing on both long edges of the bikini top (see page 9). Use a safety pin to thread both casings with elastic. Try on the bikini top, and adjust the elastic to fit. Sew the ends of the elastic together. Tie a ribbon bow around the center of the bikini top.

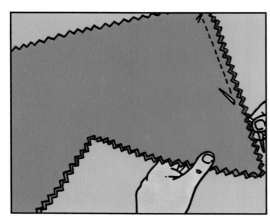

6 To make the tail, you will first need to make a full-size paper pattern following the diagram on page 87. To find out how to do this and how to cut out the pattern, read the instructions on page 8. Using pinking shears, cut out two tail shapes from the metallic fabric. Sew the tail shapes together along the side seams using running stitches (see page 8).

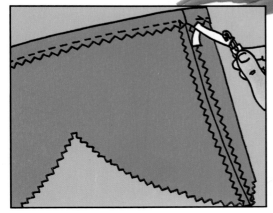

7 Make a casing on the straight top edge of the tail in the same way as you did when making the bikini top. Thread the casing with elastic. Try on the tail, and pull the ends of the elastic so that the tail fits comfortably under your knees. Sew the ends of the elastic together.

8 To finish, sew sequins to the leggings and glue shells to the bikini top and the tail.

SLEEPYHEAD

An old pair of pajamas is the main ingredient for this bedtime outfit. The nightcap is made from the pajama bottoms. To complete the sleepyhead costume, add slippers, your favorite teddy bear, and an unlit candle in a candleholder.

1 Try on the pajama top. If the sleeves are too long, cut them down to the right length. Fold under the raw edges, and stitch the new hems in place.

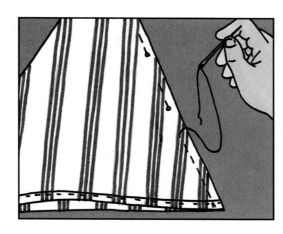

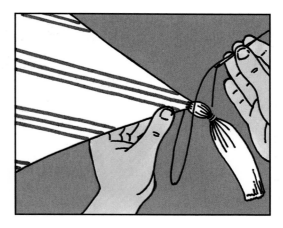

2 To make the nightcap, cut along the inside leg seams on the pajama bottoms, and lay the fabric open. Use the hemmed bottom edge of the legs as the bottom edge of your nightcap. Cut two triangles from the legs, 16½ inches wide across the bottom edge and 16½ inches along the slanted edges.

3 Pin the triangles along the slanted edges, wrong sides together. Sew the triangles together, then turn the hat right side out.

4 To finish, sew a tassel to the top of the hat. Wear the hat with the hemmed edge rolled up.

YOU WILL NEED
An old pair of adult's pajamas
Scissors; straight pins
Needle and thread
Measuring tape; pencil
A white tassel
A teddy bear
A pair of furry slippers
A candleholder and candle

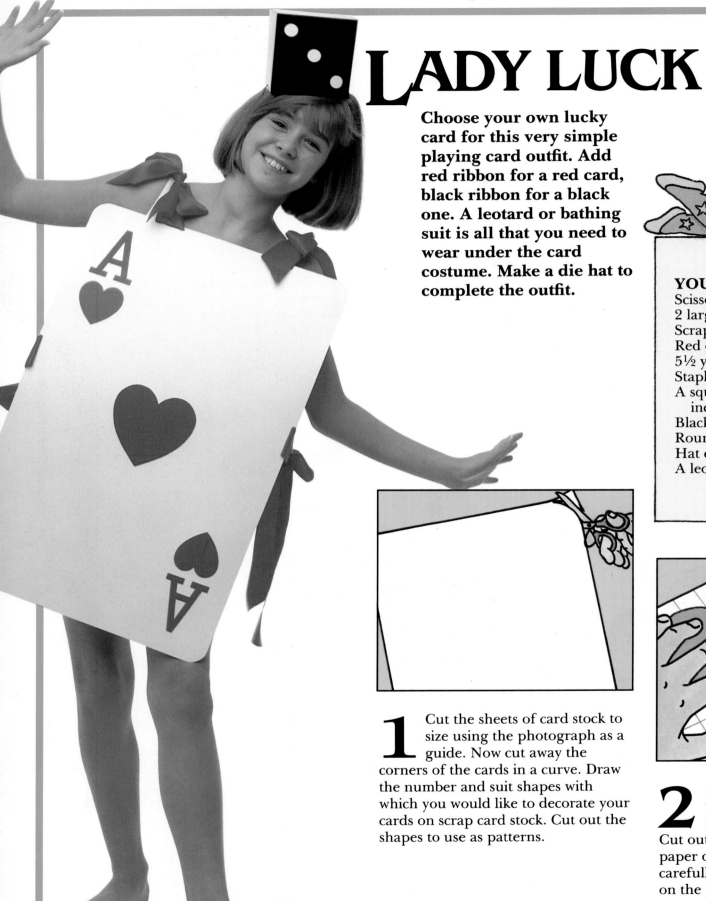

LADY LUCK

Choose your own lucky card for this very simple playing card outfit. Add red ribbon for a red card, black ribbon for a black one. A leotard or bathing suit is all that you need to wear under the card costume. Make a die hat to complete the outfit.

YOU WILL NEED
Scissors; ruler; pencil
2 large sheets of white card stock
Scrap card stock
Red or black sticky-backed plastic
5½ yards of red or black ribbon
Stapler
A square box measuring about 5½ inches on each side
Black poster paint; paintbrush
Round white stickers
Hat elastic
A leotard or bathing suit

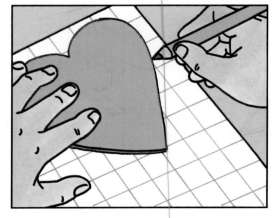

1 Cut the sheets of card stock to size using the photograph as a guide. Now cut away the corners of the cards in a curve. Draw the number and suit shapes with which you would like to decorate your cards on scrap card stock. Cut out the shapes to use as patterns.

2 Place the patterns facedown on the back of the sticky-backed plastic, and draw around them. Cut out the shapes. Peel the backing paper off the sticky-backed plastic, and carefully stick the shapes in position on the playing cards.

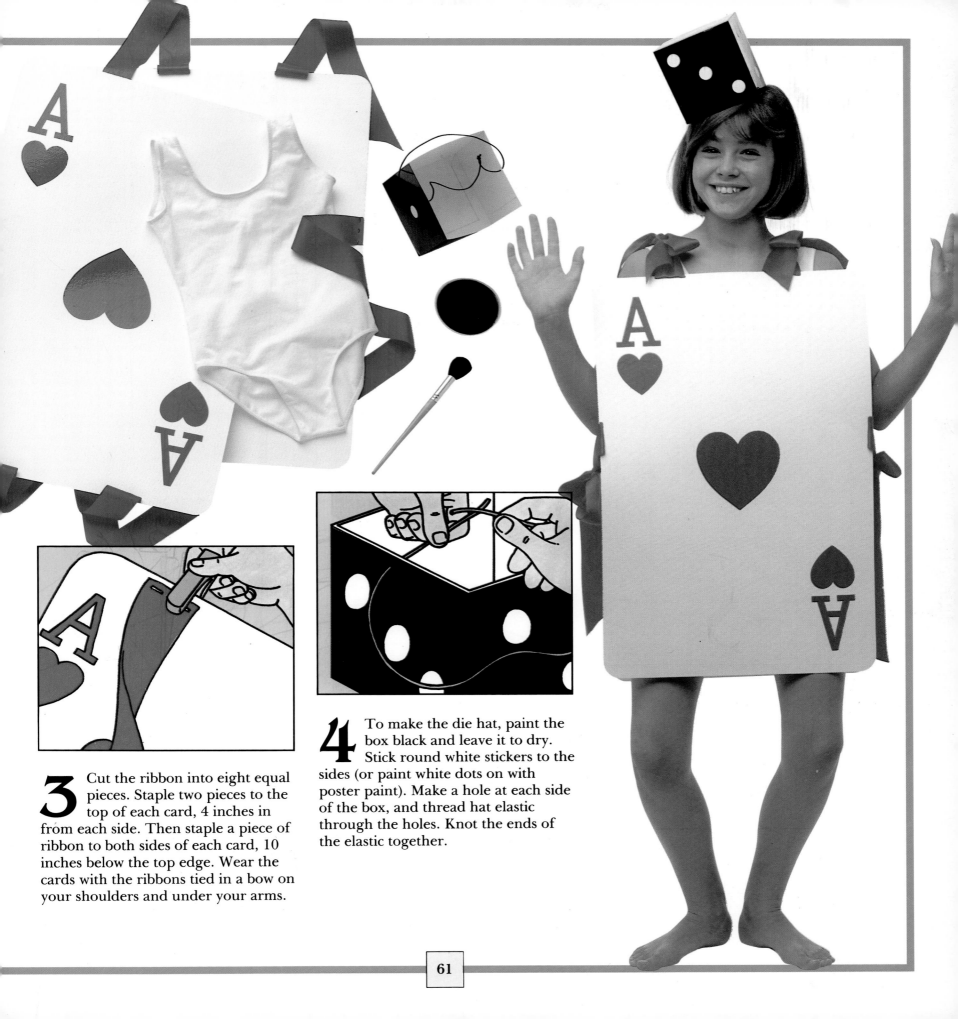

3 Cut the ribbon into eight equal pieces. Staple two pieces to the top of each card, 4 inches in from each side. Then staple a piece of ribbon to both sides of each card, 10 inches below the top edge. Wear the cards with the ribbons tied in a bow on your shoulders and under your arms.

4 To make the die hat, paint the box black and leave it to dry. Stick round white stickers to the sides (or paint white dots on with poster paint). Make a hole at each side of the box, and thread hat elastic through the holes. Knot the ends of the elastic together.

LEAPING FROG

A green body stocking or a leotard or
T-shirt and a pair of tights form the base
of this clever froggy outfit. The webbed
hands and feet are cut from vinyl, and
the flying insect is just a pipe cleaner
twisted around a candy wrapper. Make
the mask extra special by adding
joggle eyes.

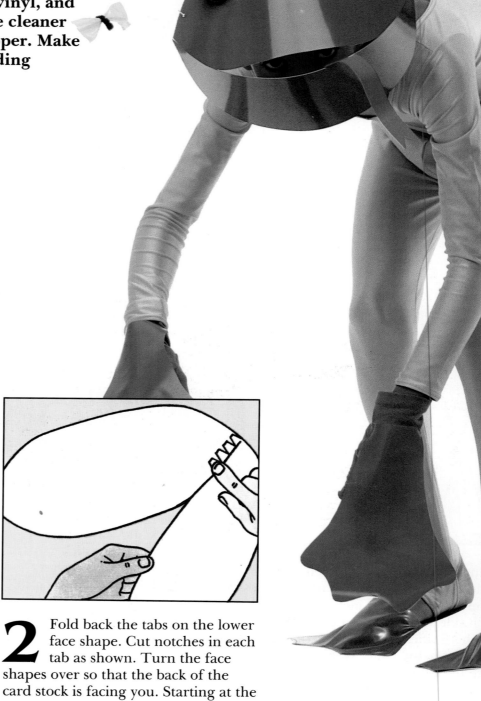

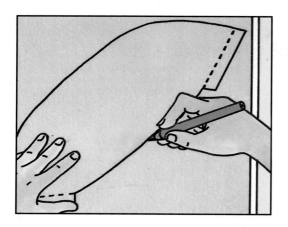

1 Using a pencil and tracing
paper, trace the upper and
lower face patterns on pages 88
and 89. Lay the tracings facedown on
the back of the green card stock. Trace
over the pencil lines to transfer the
shapes onto the card stock. Cut
them out.

2 Fold back the tabs on the lower
face shape. Cut notches in each
tab as shown. Turn the face
shapes over so that the back of the
card stock is facing you. Starting at the
corners, glue the tabs onto the lower
edge of the upper face shape.

3 Make a hole at each of the dots on the upper face, and thread the holes with hat elastic. Knot the ends inside the mask. Cut two sections from the egg carton. Paint the egg sections green, and when they are dry, glue a joggle eye to each one. Glue the egg sections to the upper face shape. Draw nostrils with a black felt-tip pen onto the upper face shape.

(Continued on the next page)

YOU WILL NEED
Pencil; tracing paper
Green and white card stock
Scissors; all-purpose glue
20 inches of hat elastic
Cardboard egg carton
Green paint; paintbrush
Two joggle eyes; black felt-tip pen
Red paper; fine wire
Black pipe cleaner; candy wrapper
Clear tape; 20 inches of 36-inch-wide green upholstery vinyl (flannel-backed vinyl)
12 inches of ½-inch-wide elastic
Needle and thread; green gloves
A green body stocking

SAFETY TIP: *Make sure an adult helps you when using wire.*

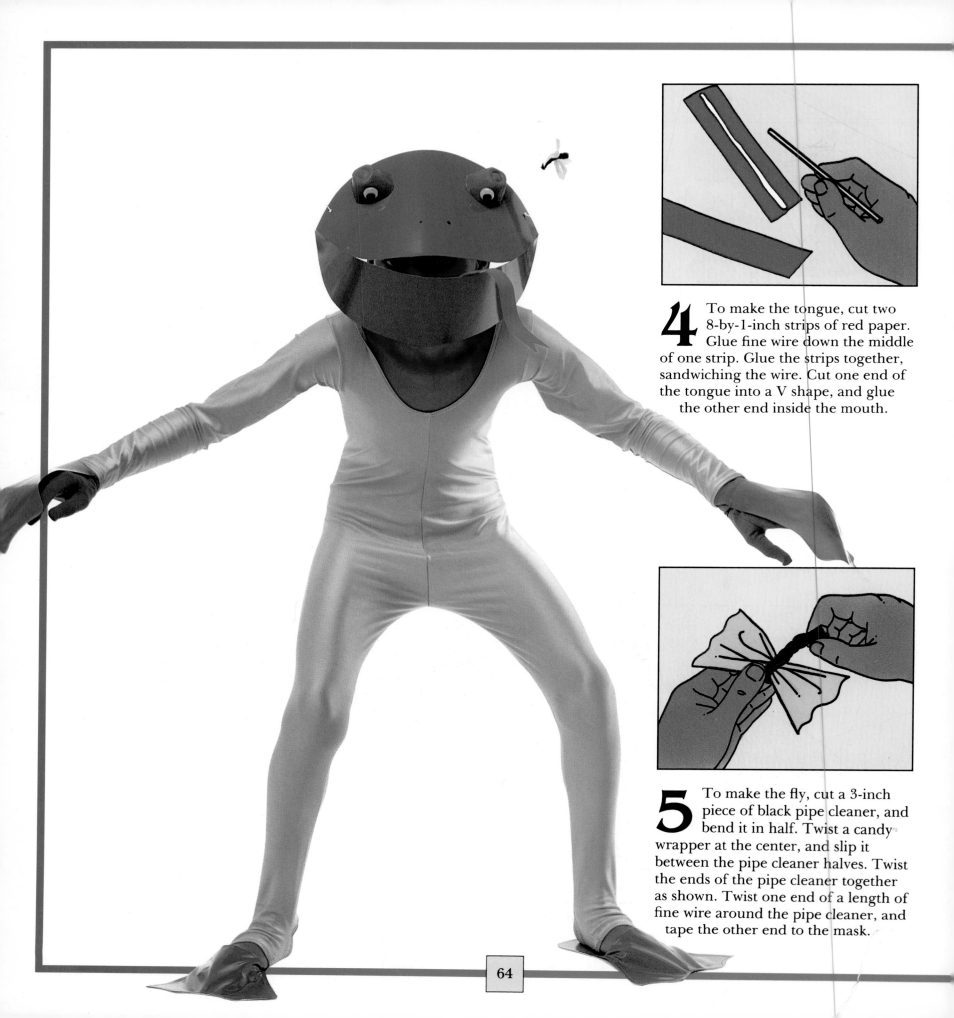

4 To make the tongue, cut two 8-by-1-inch strips of red paper. Glue fine wire down the middle of one strip. Glue the strips together, sandwiching the wire. Cut one end of the tongue into a V shape, and glue the other end inside the mouth.

5 To make the fly, cut a 3-inch piece of black pipe cleaner, and bend it in half. Twist a candy wrapper at the center, and slip it between the pipe cleaner halves. Twist the ends of the pipe cleaner together as shown. Twist one end of a length of fine wire around the pipe cleaner, and tape the other end to the mask.

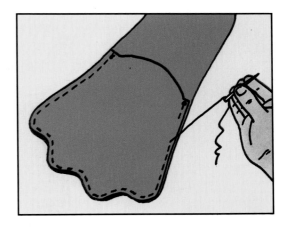

8 Stitch the shoe uppers to the vinyl shoe soles, carefully matching the dots shown on the patterns. To finish, glue the card stock soles under the vinyl soles.

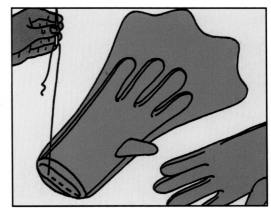

9 To make the webbed hands, trace the pattern on page 92 and cut it out. Tape the pattern onto a double layer of vinyl, and cut out two hand shapes. Sew the hands to the back of the gloves.

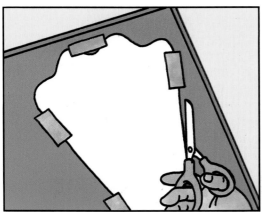

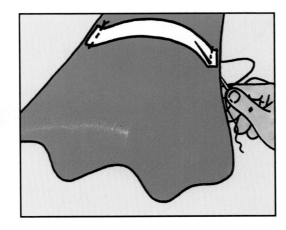

6 To make the webbed shoes, trace the upper and sole patterns on pages 90 and 91. Lay the shoe sole pattern facedown on white card stock. Trace over the pencil lines to transfer the shape onto the card stock. Cut the sole out. Now lay the shape back on the card stock, trace around it, and cut out another shoe sole. Lay one of the soles on a double layer of green vinyl, and hold it in place with clear tape. Cut out two vinyl soles.

7 Cut two 4½-inch lengths of the wide elastic. Stitch each end to the vinyl soles at the dots shown on the pattern. Wear the shoes with the elastic over your feet. Now cut out the tracing for the webbed shoe upper. Tape it to a double layer of green vinyl, and cut out two shoe uppers.

VAMPIRE

Large squares of black and red satin stitched together make a splendid cloak for this stunning outfit. Underneath it wear a plain white shirt and black or dark gray pants, dressed up with a ribbon sash. For added effect, make a black top hat and wear a pair of fangs.

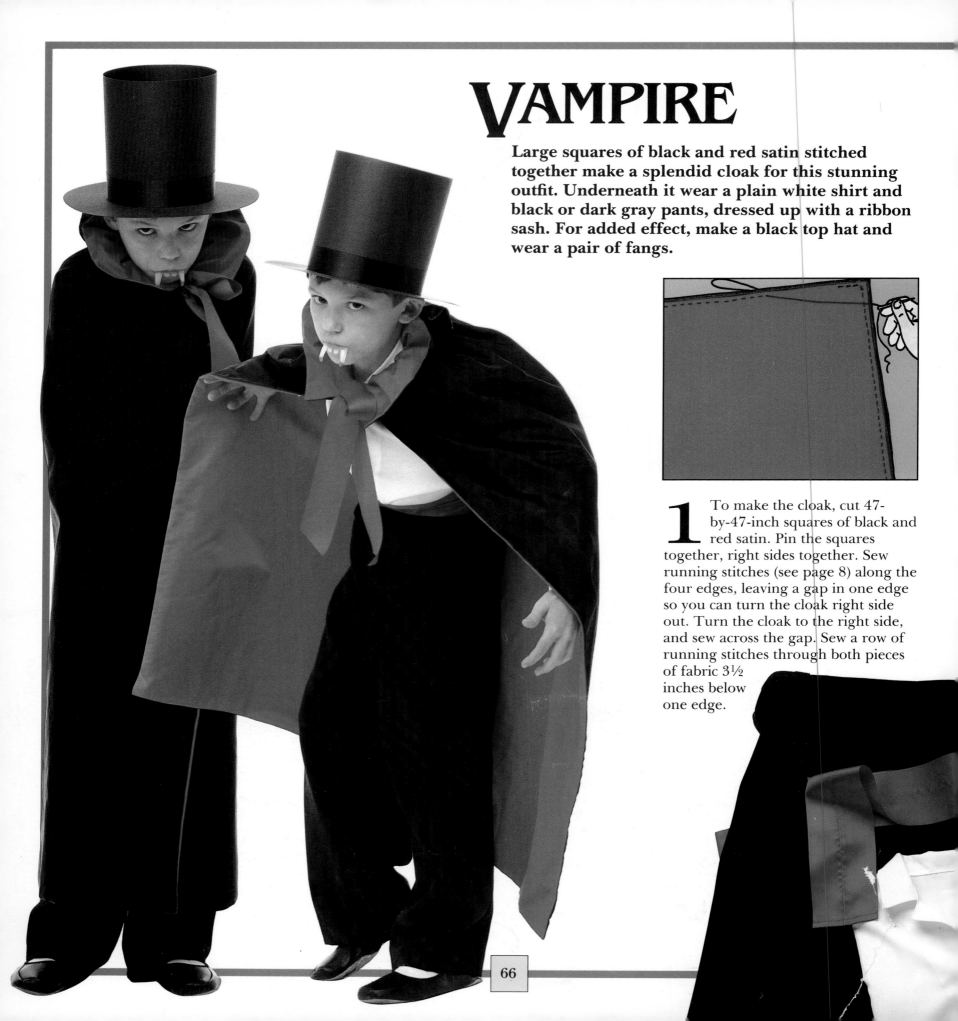

1 To make the cloak, cut 47-by-47-inch squares of black and red satin. Pin the squares together, right sides together. Sew running stitches (see page 8) along the four edges, leaving a gap in one edge so you can turn the cloak right side out. Turn the cloak to the right side, and sew across the gap. Sew a row of running stitches through both pieces of fabric 3½ inches below one edge.

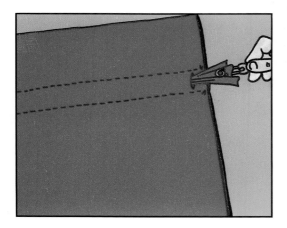

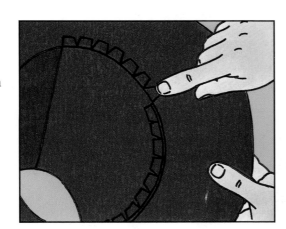

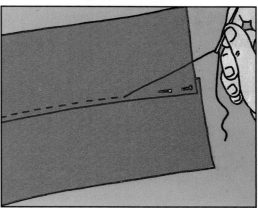

YOU WILL NEED

1½ yards each of 60-inch-wide
    red and black satin
Measuring tape; fabric marker
Scissors
Straight pins; needle and thread
3¼ yards of wide mauve ribbon
Safety pin
Black card stock
Pencil; ruler; glue; compass
24 inches of wide black ribbon
Plastic fangs (from a joke shop)
Old white shirt; black pants
Black shoes

2 Sew another row of stitches 1 inch below the first row to make a casing. Carefully cut a slit between the rows of stitching at each end of the casing. Cut a 63-inch-long piece of mauve ribbon. Attach a safety pin to one end. Thread the pin through the casing. Feel for the pin through the fabric, and ease it through the casing. Remove the pin. You'll tie the ribbon in a bow to secure the cloak when you wear it.

3 To make the hat, cut a 22-by-8-inch strip of black card stock. Draw a line ⅝ inch above one long edge. Fold the card stock along the line, and cut tabs along the edge as shown. Form the strip into a tube shape, and glue the long edges together. This is the crown of the hat.

4 To make the hat brim, cut out a circle of black card stock with a diameter of 12 inches. Stand the straight edge of the crown in the middle of the circle, and trace around it. Cut out the circle. Slip the hat brim over the crown, and glue the snipped edge under the brim. Glue black ribbon around the hat for a hatband.

5 Cut the remaining piece of mauve ribbon in half lengthwise to make a sash. Overlap the long edges, and stitch them together. To finish, make a hem at each end (see page 9). Tie the sash around your waist.

MENACING MONSTER

Make this monster costume as fearsome as possible by sewing pieces of bubble wrap to the body stocking to look like scales and making bubble wrap humps to attach to the back. If you don't have a body stocking, a leotard or T-shirt and a pair of leggings or tights will work just as well.

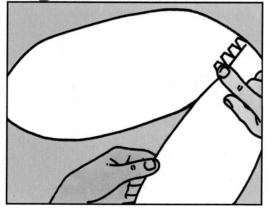

1 Using a pencil and tracing paper, trace the upper and lower face patterns on pages 88 and 89. Lay the tracings facedown on the back of the purple card stock. Trace over the pencil lines to transfer the shapes onto the card stock. Cut the patterns out. Fold back the tabs on the lower face shape. Cut notches in each tab as shown.

2 Turn the face shapes over so the back of the card stock is facing you. Starting at the corners, glue the tabs along the lower edge of the upper face shape. Make a hole at each of the dots on the upper face. Thread each hole with hat elastic. Knot the elastic inside the mask. Glue the eyes to the upper face shape.

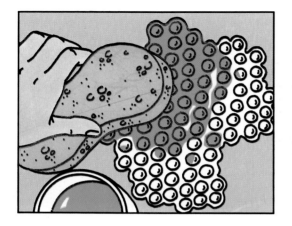

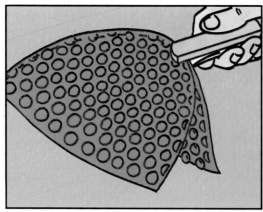

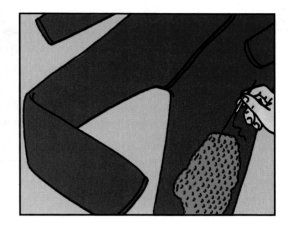

3 Put some green paint into a shallow dish. Using a sponge, dab paint onto pieces of bubble wrap, then leave it to dry. Cut out shapes from the bubble wrap, and glue them to the mask. Cut out some more shapes to attach to the body stocking later.

4 To make the humps, cut two circles with 6-inch diameters from bubble wrap. Cut the circles in half, and staple the half circles together as shown. Leave the bottom edge open. Crumple up some tissue paper, and stuff it into the humps.

5 Try on the body stocking and fix safety pins to the places where you want to attach the pieces of bubble wrap and the humps. Ask an adult to help you do this. Take off the body stocking. Attach the bubble wrap pieces and the humps to the body stocking with a few stitches. Paint a piece of scrap card stock green, and cut six triangles for claws. Sew or glue three claws to the toe of each sock.

YOU WILL NEED
Tracing paper; pencil
Purple card stock; scissors
All-purpose glue
32 inches of hat elastic
2 funny fake eyes (from a toy store)
Green poster paint
Shallow dish; sponge
Bubble wrap; compass; stapler
Green tissue paper; safety pins
A purple body stocking (or a leotard and tights); needle and thread
A pair of purple socks

CRAZY CLOWN

You'll be the center of attention in this colorful clown costume. Decorate the shirt with glitter paints and make suspenders from bright red ribbon. To complete your outfit, make a glittery hat, a pair of extra-large shoes, and a big bow tie.

YOU WILL NEED
An adult's old shirt
Scissors; plastic bags
Glitter paints and paintbrush
 (or glitter pens)
2 rubber bands
A pair of old tracksuit pants
A 40-inch length of plastic boning
Needle and thread
2½ yards of wide ribbon
4 large buttons
Measuring tape; fabric pencil
A Ping-Pong ball
2¼ yards of hat elastic

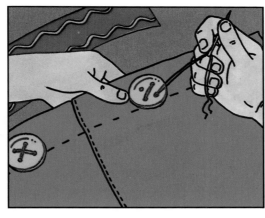

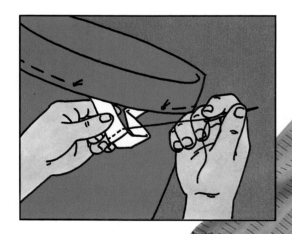

1 Cut the cuffs off the shirtsleeves. Slip a plastic bag into the end of each sleeve, and decorate the bottom of the sleeves with glitter paints. Wear the shirt with rubber bands slipped over the wrists to gather the sleeves.

2 Carefully unpick a few stitches from the waistband of the pants, and knot the snipped ends. Then pull out the elastic from the waistband. Push the boning into the waistband casing until it comes out the other end. Sew the ends of the boning together.

3 To make the suspenders, cut the ribbon in half and decorate both halves with glitter paints. Sew two buttons to the front of the pants and two to the back 3 inches from either side of the front and back seams. Cut a slit in one end of each of the ribbons and fasten them on the buttons on the back of the pants.

YOU WILL ALSO NEED

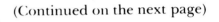

Ruler; pencil
Red metallic crepe paper
Clear tape; all-pupose glue
Tracing paper
Yellow card stock
3 red pompoms
Narrow gift-wrap ribbon
16 inches of 36-inch-wide yellow
  upholstery vinyl (flannel-backed
  vinyl)
12 inches of ½-inch-wide elastic
Straight pins

(Continued on the next page)

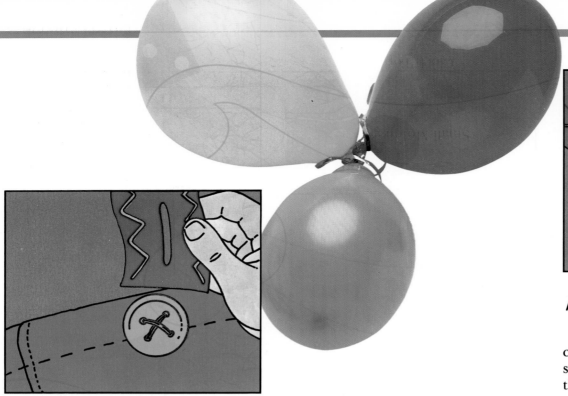

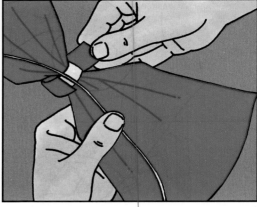

7 Place a length of hat elastic across the back of the bow tie. Wrap a narrow strip of metallic crepe paper around the middle, and secure it with glue. Knot the ends of the elastic together at the back of your neck.

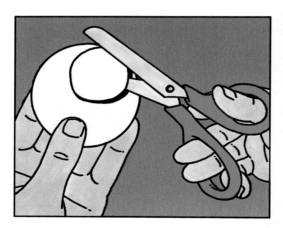

4 Try the pants on, and pull the suspenders over your shoulders. Cut slits in the other ends of the suspenders, and fasten them to the front buttons.

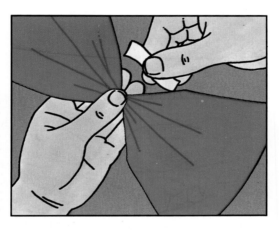

6 Cut a 12-by-6½-inch rectangle of metallic crepe paper for the bow tie and two 8-by-5-inch rectangles for the shoe bows. Squeeze the rectangles in the middle to make bows, and bind each with clear tape. Decorate the bows with glitter paints.

5 To make the nose, cut a hole in the Ping-Pong ball large enough to fit over your nose. Paint the ball with glitter paint, and leave it to dry. Make a hole at each side of the ball and thread hat elastic through the holes. Knot the elastic at the back of your head.

8 Trace the hat pattern on pages 94 and 95, and lay it facedown on yellow card stock. Trace over the pencil lines to transfer the pattern onto the card stock. Cut the hat out, and decorate it with glitter paints. Overlap and glue the straight edges. Glue on pompoms. Make a hole at each side of the hat, and thread hat elastic through. Knot it inside. Glue gift-wrap ribbon inside the hat.

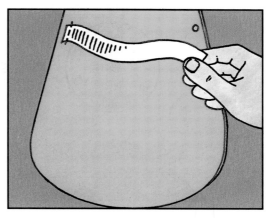

10 Cut two 4½-inch lengths of wide elastic. Stitch each end to the vinyl soles at the dots shown on the pattern. Wear the shoes with the elastic over your feet. Now cut out the tracing for the shoe upper. Tape it onto a double layer of yellow vinyl, and cut out two shoe uppers.

9 To make the shoes, trace the upper and sole patterns on pages 93 and 94. Lay the shoe sole tracing facedown on card stock. Trace over the pencil lines to transfer the pattern onto the card stock. Cut the sole out. Now lay the shape back on the card stock. Trace around it, and cut out another shoe sole. Lay one of the soles on a double layer of yellow vinyl, and hold it in place with clear tape. Cut out two vinyl soles.

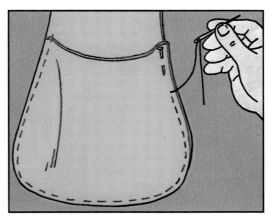

11 Stitch the uppers to the vinyl soles, matching the soles to the uppers at the dots shown on the patterns. Glue the card stock soles under the vinyl soles. Glue the shoe bows to the shoes.

CHRISTMAS TREE

Why go to a party as a Christmas present when you can dress up as the whole tree? The basic cape and skirt are made from green metallic crepe paper gathered on a sticky-backed plastic waistband and neckband. Once you have made the treetop hat, you can trim the outfit with lots of tinsel, ornaments, and other decorations.

1 To make the waistband, cut a strip of sticky-backed plastic 1½ inches wide and long enough to fit around your waist plus 2 inches. Cut another strip 15½ inches long by 1½ inches wide for the neckband. Stick double-sided tape along one long edge of the backing paper of the waistband and the neckband. Do not remove the backing paper from the sticky-backed plastic.

YOU WILL NEED
Scissors; tape measure
Gold or silver sticky-backed plastic
Double-sided tape
Green metallic crepe paper
Stick-on Velcro
Tracing paper; pencil
Thin card stock
All-purpose glue
28 inches of hat elastic
Lightweight Christmas garland and ornaments
Needle and thread
Clear tape
A green body stocking (or a leotard or T-shirt and tights)

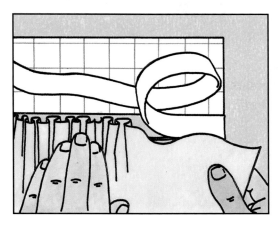

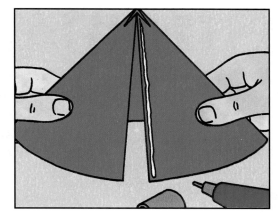

2 Cut two 70-by-12-inch strips of metallic crepe paper. These are for the skirt and the cape. To make the skirt, gradually peel the backing paper off the double-sided tape on the waistband and stick the long edge of one strip of crepe paper to the tape. Gather the crepe paper to fit. Fasten the ends of the waistband with Velcro. Join the cape to the neckband in the same way.

3 To make the hat, trace the pattern on pages 94 and 95. Lay the tracing facedown on thin card stock. Trace over the pencil lines to transfer the shape onto the card stock. Cut the hat out. Glue metallic crepe paper to the shape, and trim the edges. Cut slits in the top of the hat as shown on the pattern. Form the hat into a cone, overlapping the straight edges, and glue them together.

4 Make a hole at the bottom of each side of the hat, and thread hat elastic through the holes. Knot the ends of the elastic over the holes. Stick gold sticky-backed plastic to both sides of a piece of card stock, and cut out a star shape. Fit the star into the slit at the top of the hat. Glue a garland around the bottom of the hat.

5 Drape garlands around the skirt and cape, and stitch them in place. Sew tree decorations to the hat, skirt, and cape. Stick tape over the stitching on the wrong side of the crepe paper so that the paper doesn't tear. Wrap a length of garland around each wrist, and ask a friend to stick the ends together with tape.

MORE COSTUME IDEAS

Once you have made some of the costumes featured in this book, why not try creating your own original outfits by adapting the patterns found here? On these pages we have suggested ways that you can adapt some of the costumes by using different colored materials and adding matching accessories.

MOUSE

Nose made from a Ping-Pong ball painted black; glue whiskers to the nose

Pink and gray felt ears sewn onto a headband

White body stocking or a pair of white leggings and a T-shirt

White gloves

BLACK CAT Page 44

Tail made from a length of rope

WICKED WITCH Page 50

WIZARD

Black felt hat decorated with stars and moons cut from yellow felt

Green nightgown

Green hair made from yarn

RABBIT

Pink and gray card stock ears glued to a headband

Nose made from a Ping-Pong ball painted black; glue whiskers to the nose

White card stock teeth

White gloves

Gray body stocking or a pair of gray leggings and a T-shirt

Fluffy tail made from cotton

Black cloak decorated with stars and moons cut from yellow felt

SOUTHERN BELLE Page **22**

GYPSY PRINCESS

Curtain rings for earrings

White T-shirt

Shawl or scarf

Green skirt made from plastic trash bags trimmed with gold braid

PENCIL PERSON
Page **52**

FLOWER

FIRECRACKER

Card stock cone hat decorated with glitter pens

Brightly colored crepe paper petals attached to elastic

Card stock body shape decorated with poster paints and glitter pens

Green crepe paper leaves glued to body shape

Green card stock body shape for the stem

Crepe paper frill

PATTERNS

The following pages show the patterns and templates you will need to make many of the projects in the book. To find out how to copy a pattern, follow the step-by-step instructions given for each project.

Some of the patterns are shown as diagrams with measurements so that you can draw the correct size pattern piece on paper. To find out how to do this, follow the instructions for Making a Paper Pattern on page 8.

The patterns have all been designed to fit an average nine-year-old or ten-year-old. Before cutting out the fabric, check that the measurements given with the patterns are correct for you. If necessary, change the size of the pattern pieces to fit.

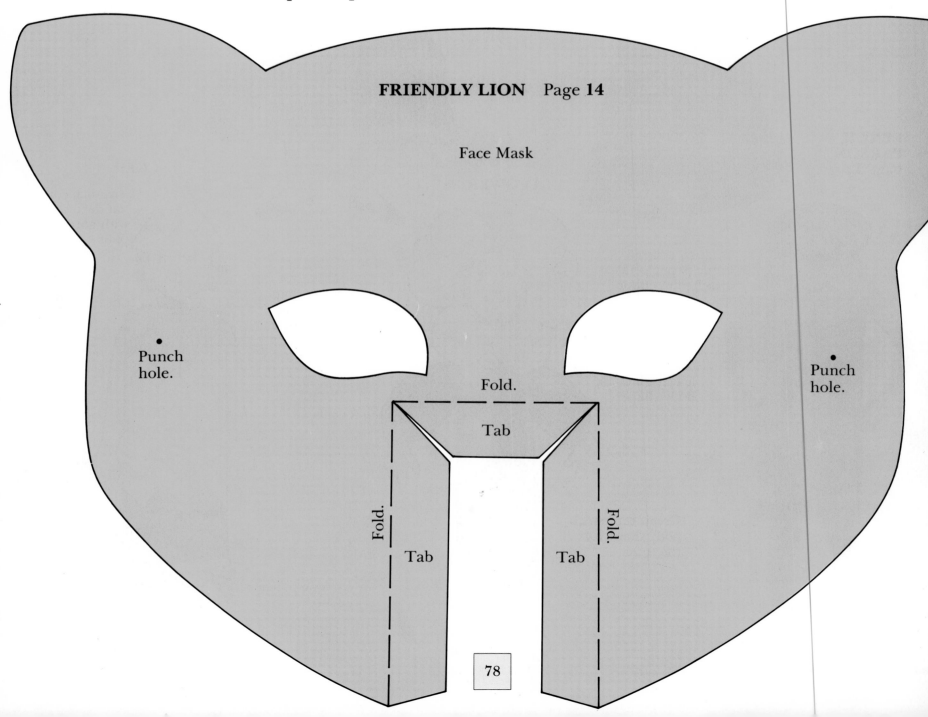

FRIENDLY LION   Page **14**

Face Mask

Punch hole.

Punch hole.

Fold.

Tab

Fold.

Fold.

Tab

Tab

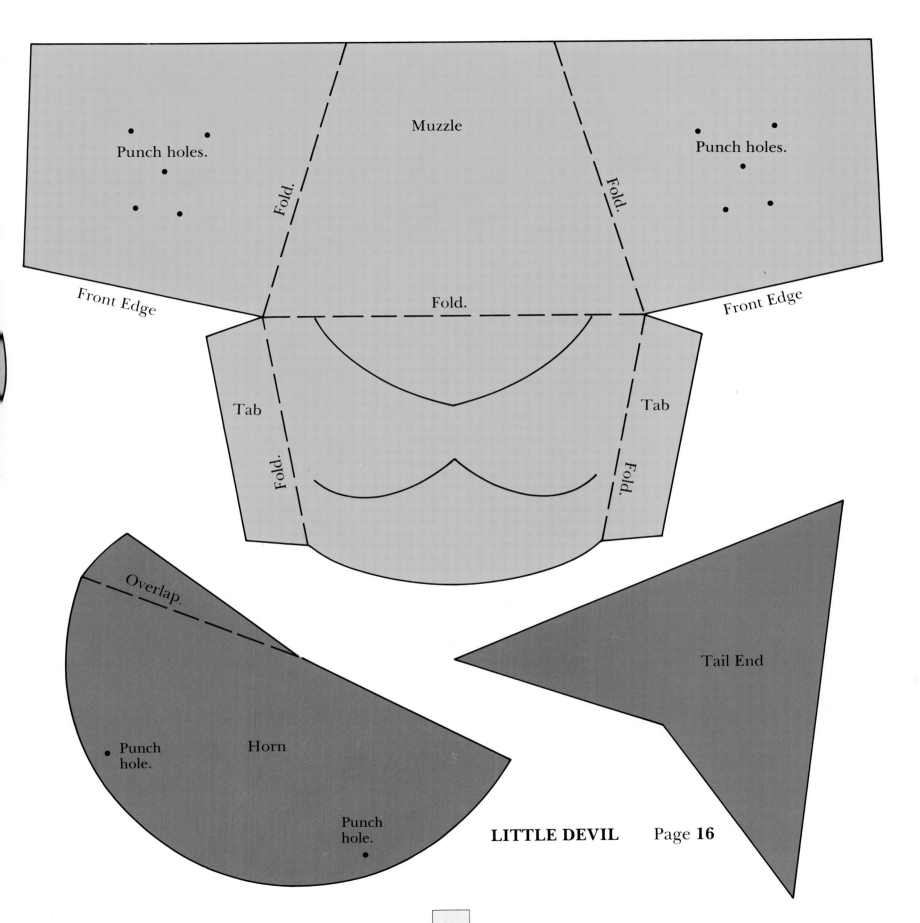

Muzzle

Punch holes.

Punch holes.

Fold.

Fold.

Front Edge

Fold.

Front Edge

Tab

Tab

Fold.

Fold.

Overlap.

Tail End

Punch hole.

Horn

Punch hole.

LITTLE DEVIL   Page **16**

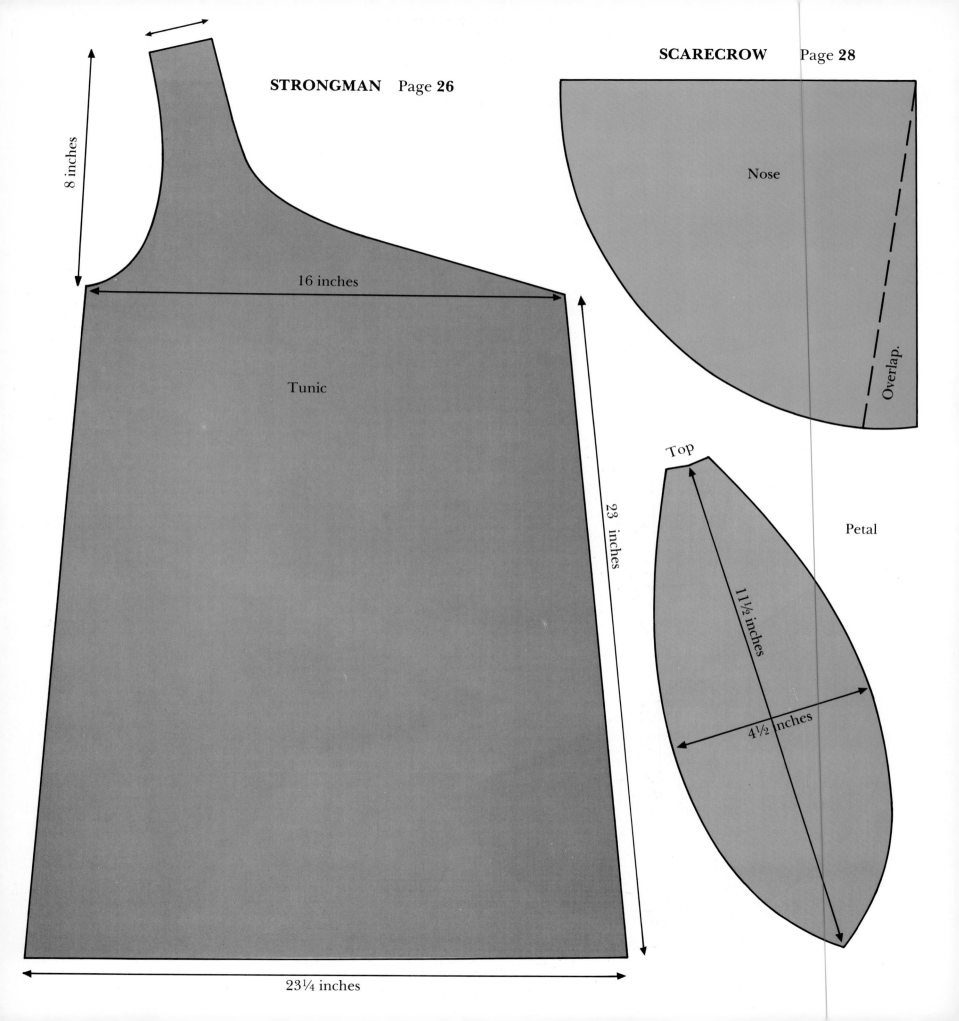

STRONGMAN   Page **26**

8 inches

16 inches

Tunic

23 inches

23¼ inches

SCARECROW   Page **28**

Nose

Overlap.

Top

Petal

11½ inches

4½ inches

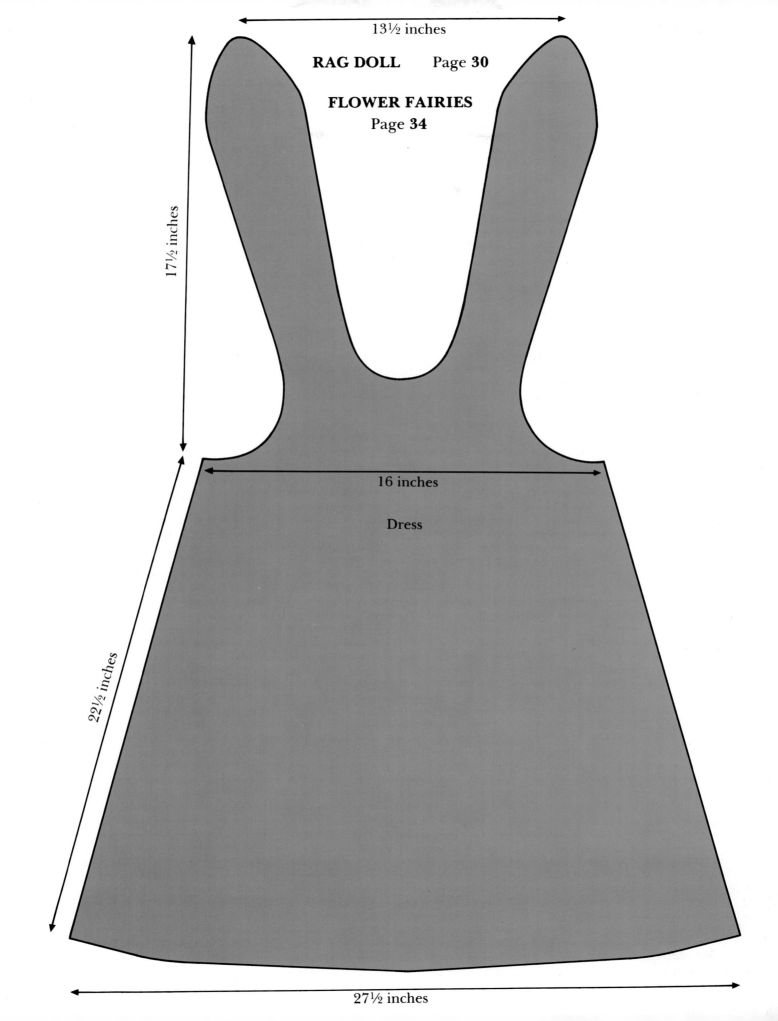

13½ inches

RAG DOLL   Page **30**

FLOWER FAIRIES
Page **34**

17½ inches

16 inches

Dress

22½ inches

27½ inches

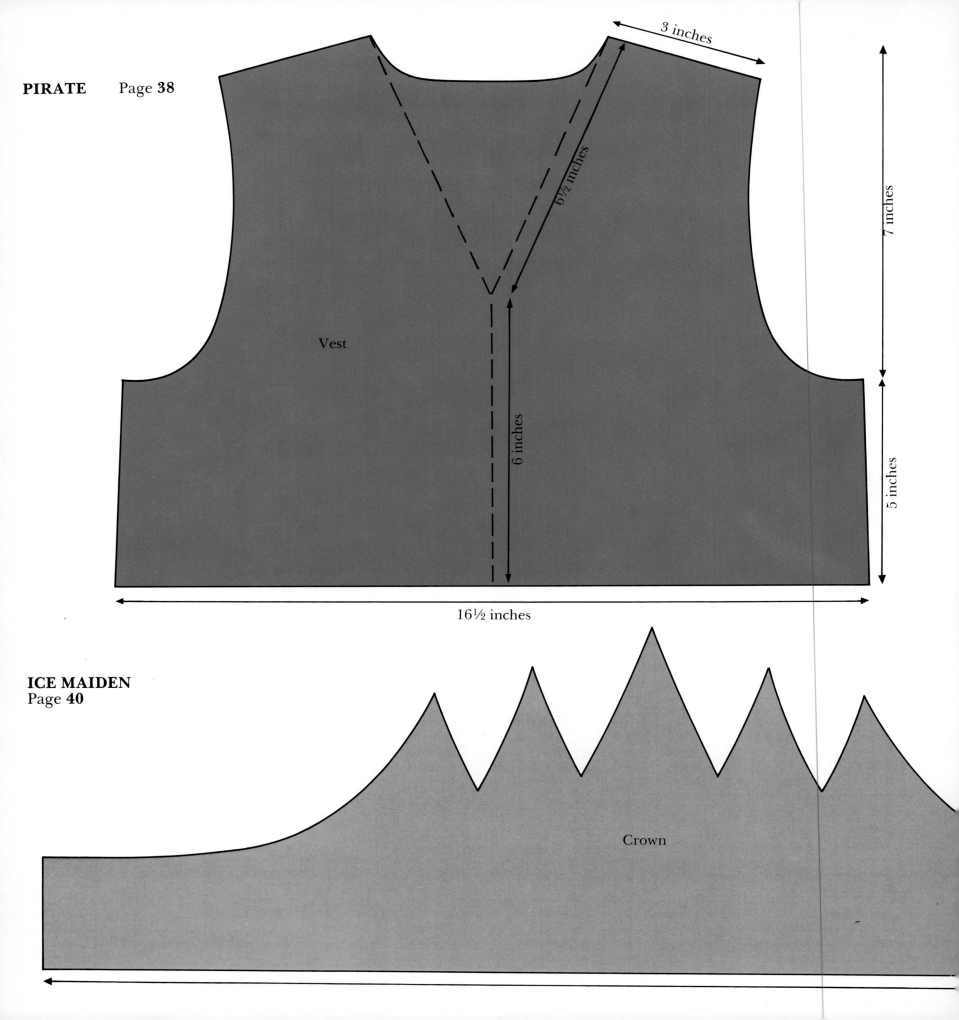

PIRATE   Page **38**

3 inches

7 inches

6½ inches

Vest

6 inches

5 inches

16½ inches

ICE MAIDEN
Page **40**

Crown

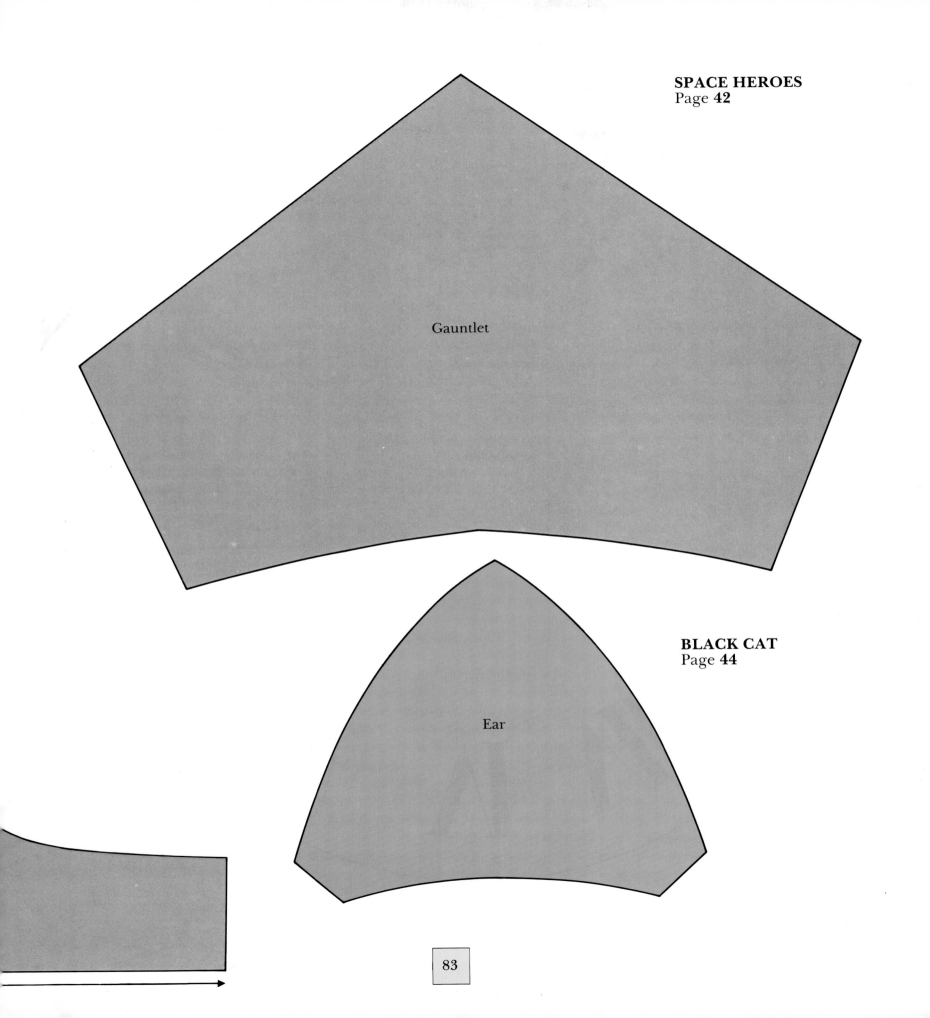

Gauntlet

Ear

Hand

Hand

Clock Face

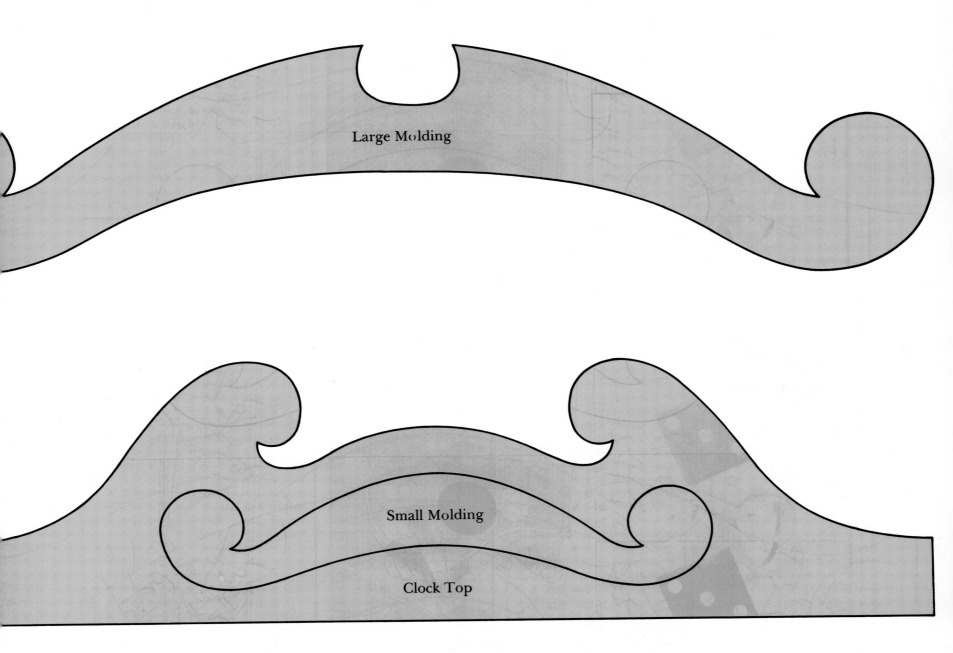

Large Molding

Small Molding

Clock Top

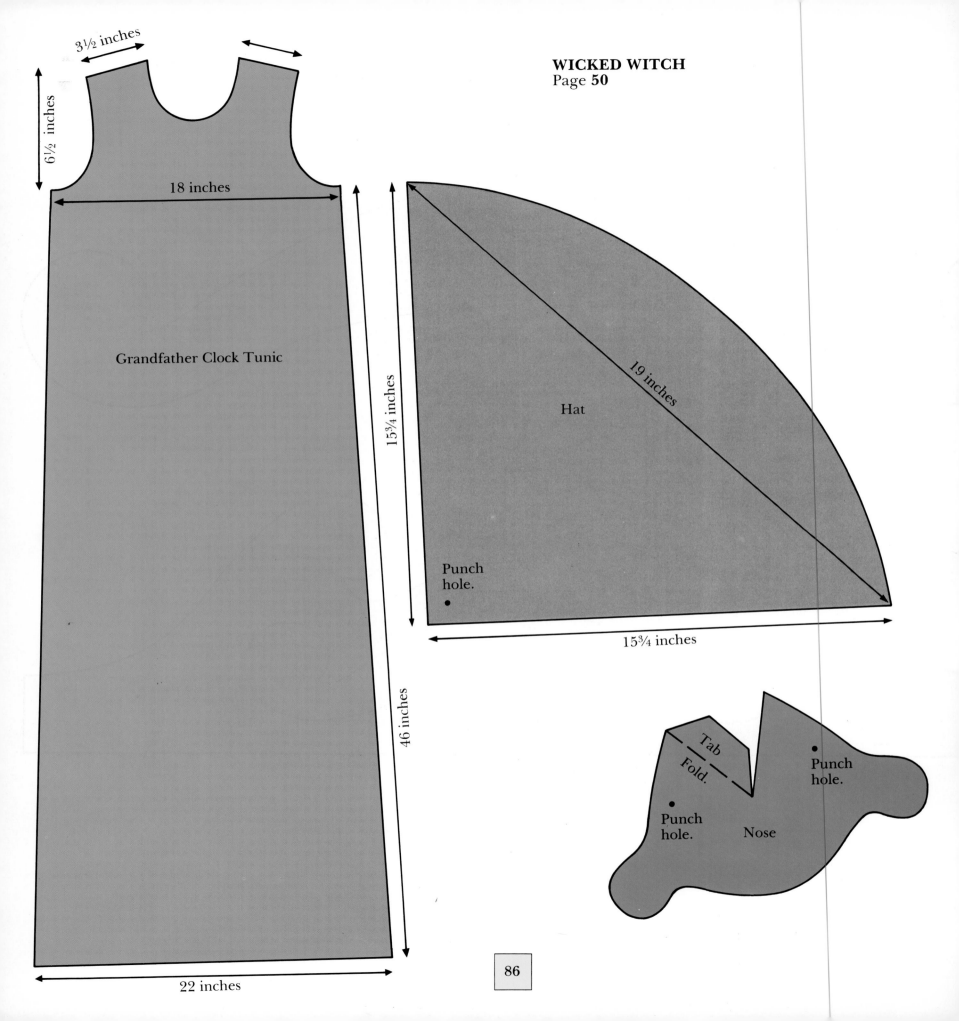

3½ inches

6½ inches

18 inches

Grandfather Clock Tunic

15¾ inches

46 inches

22 inches

Hat

19 inches

15¾ inches

Punch hole.

Tab

Fold.

Punch hole.

Punch hole.

Nose

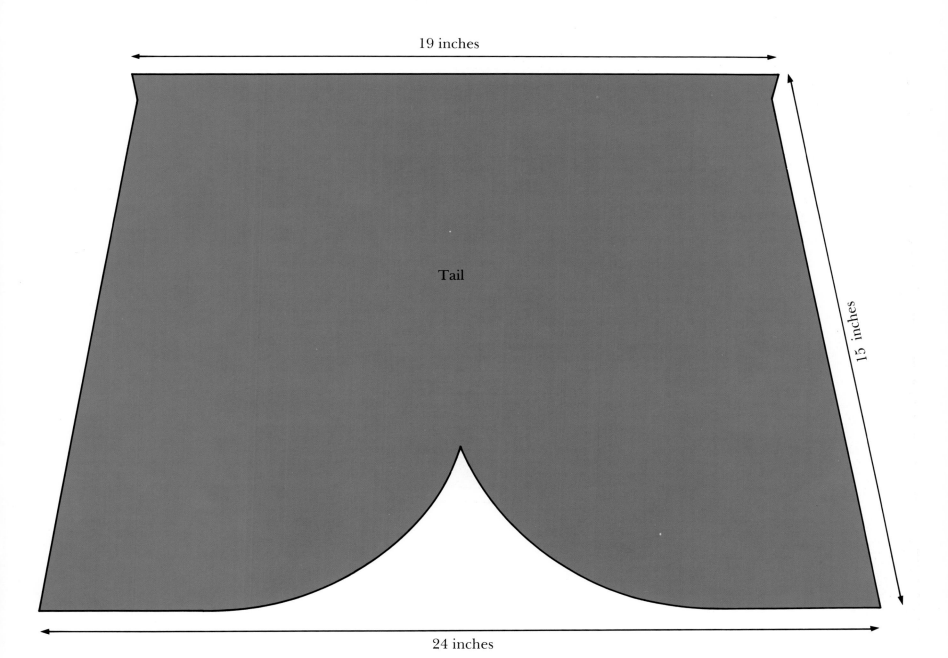

19 inches

15 inches

Tail

24 inches

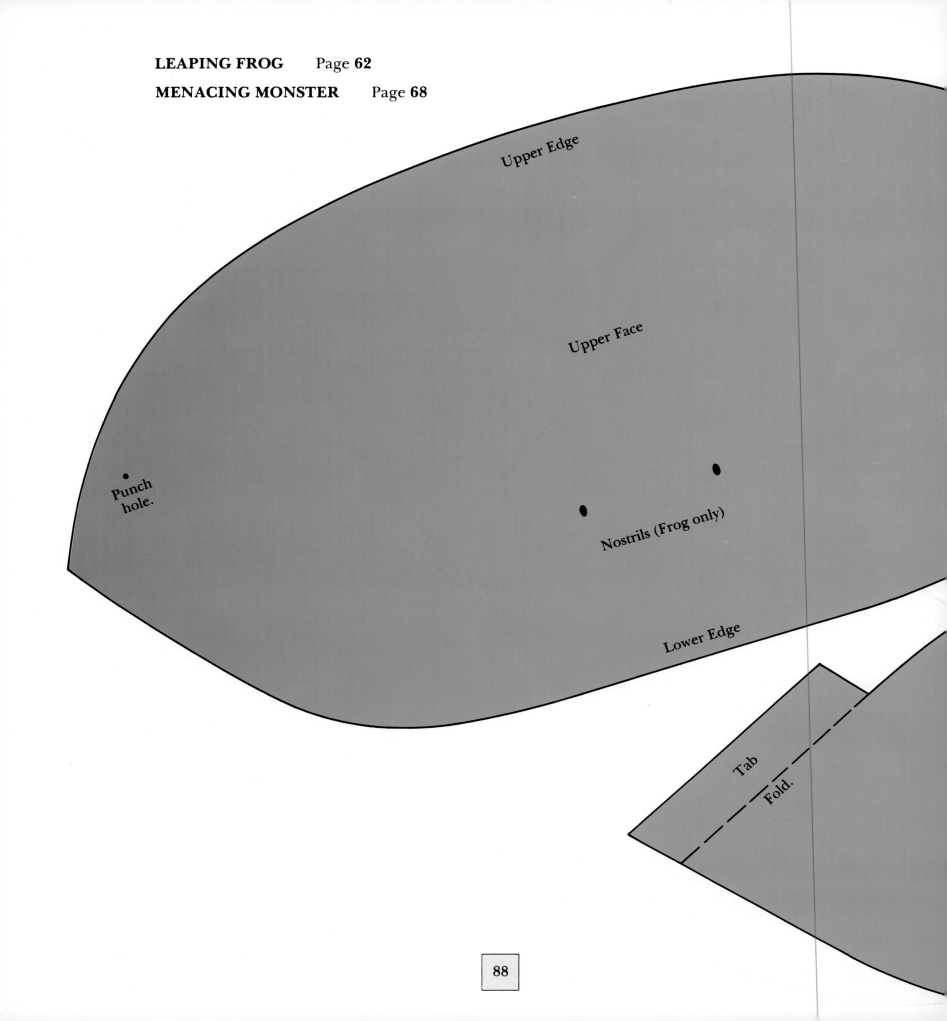

Upper Edge

Upper Face

Punch hole.

Nostrils (Frog only)

Lower Edge

Tab

Fold.

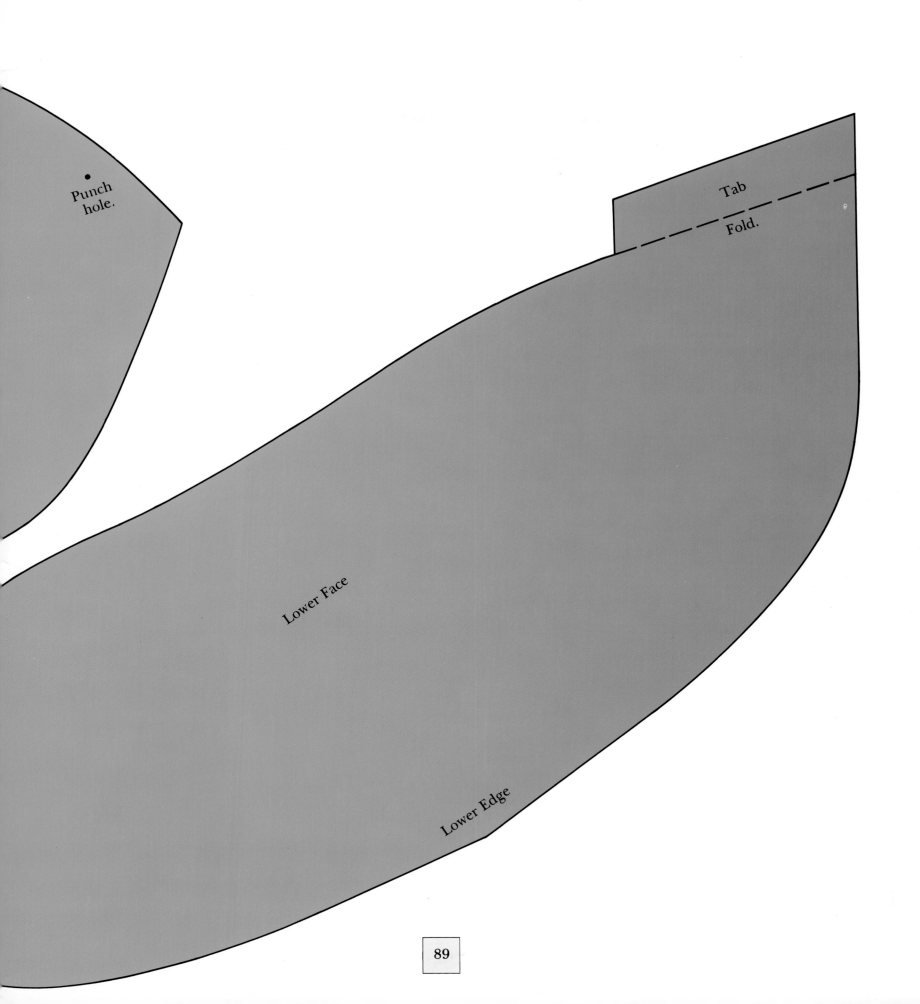

Punch
hole.

Tab

Fold.

Lower Face

Lower Edge

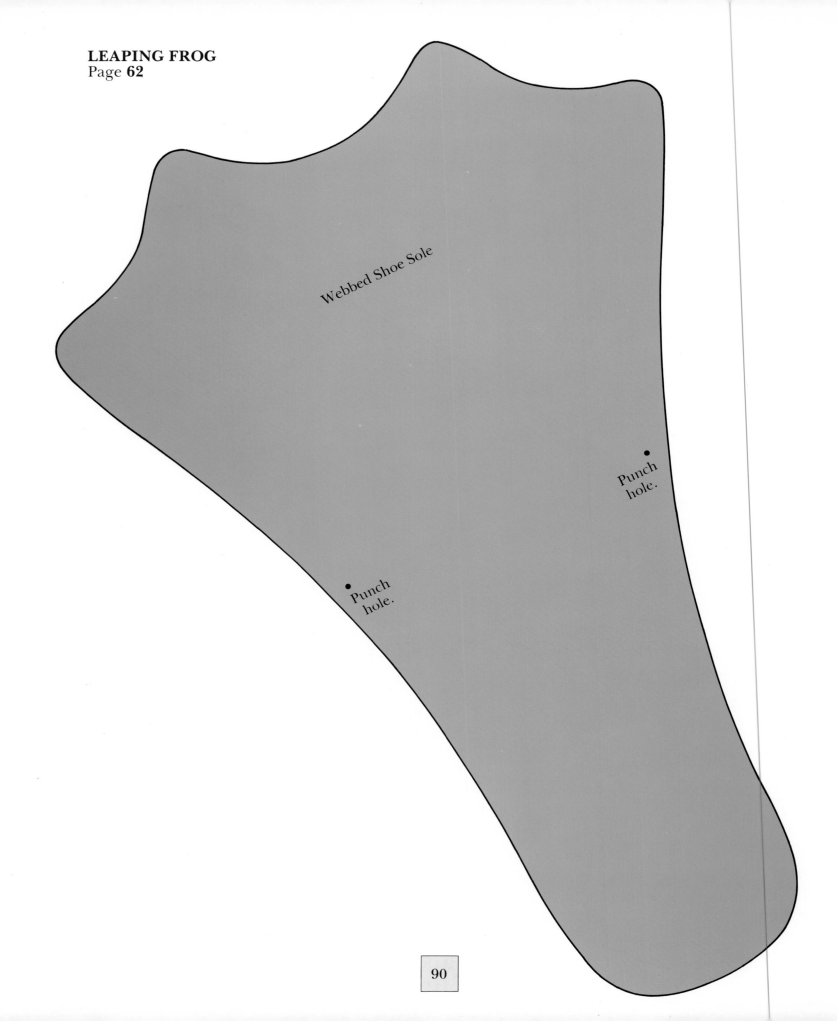

Webbed Shoe Sole

Punch hole.

Punch hole.

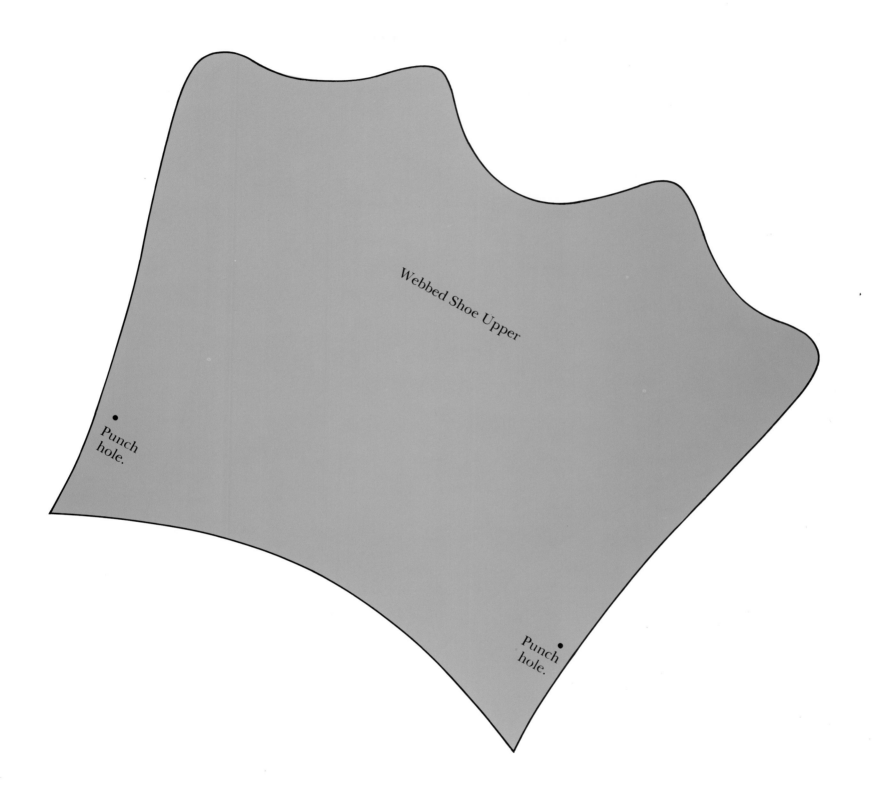

Webbed Shoe Upper

Punch hole.

Punch
hole.

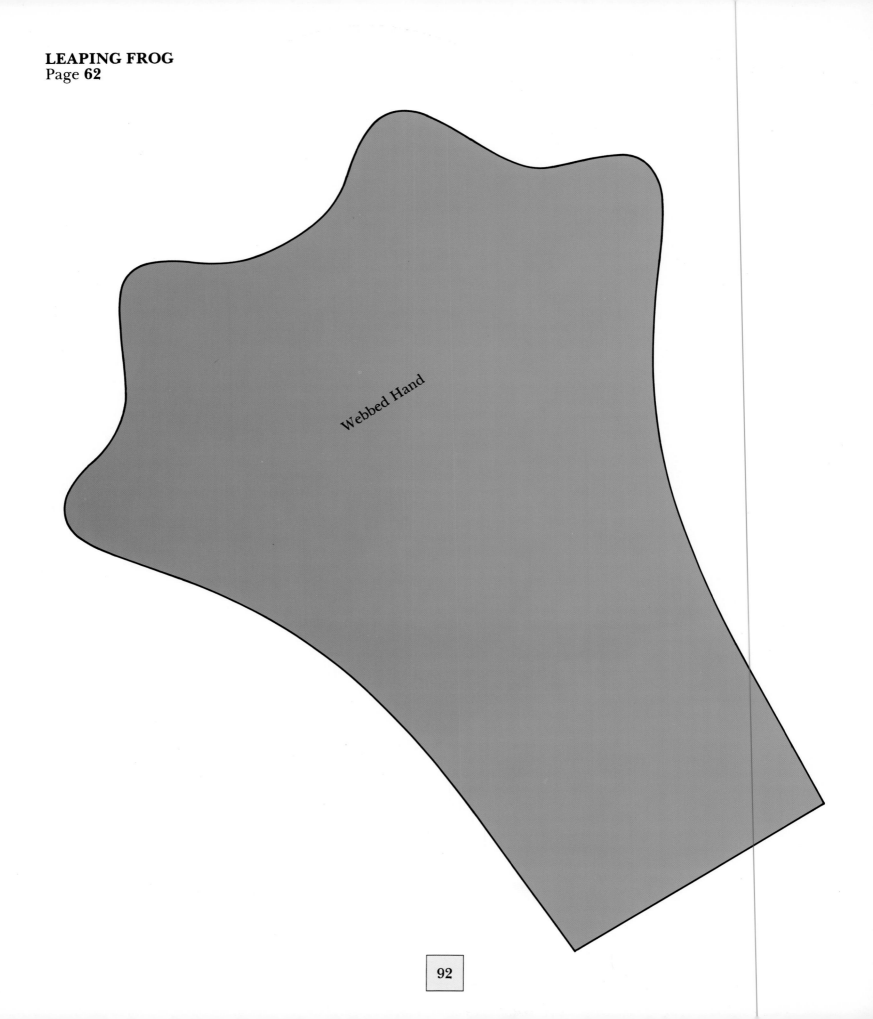

Webbed Hand

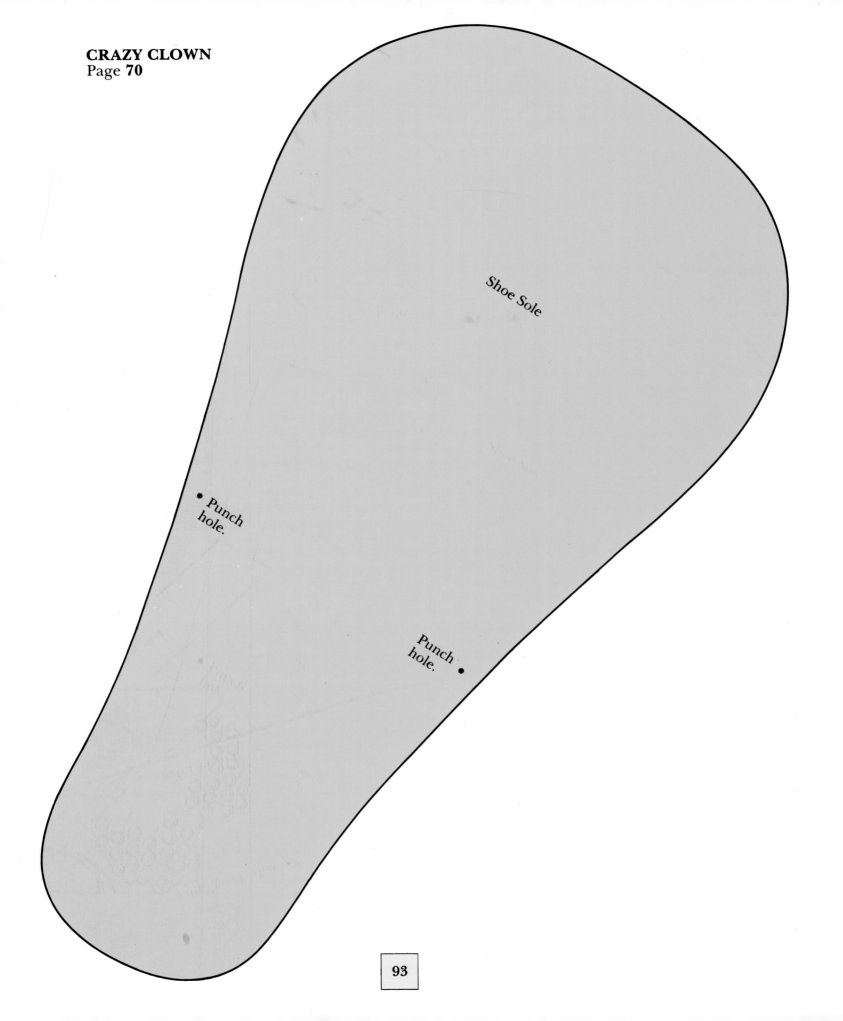

Shoe Sole

Punch hole.

Punch hole.

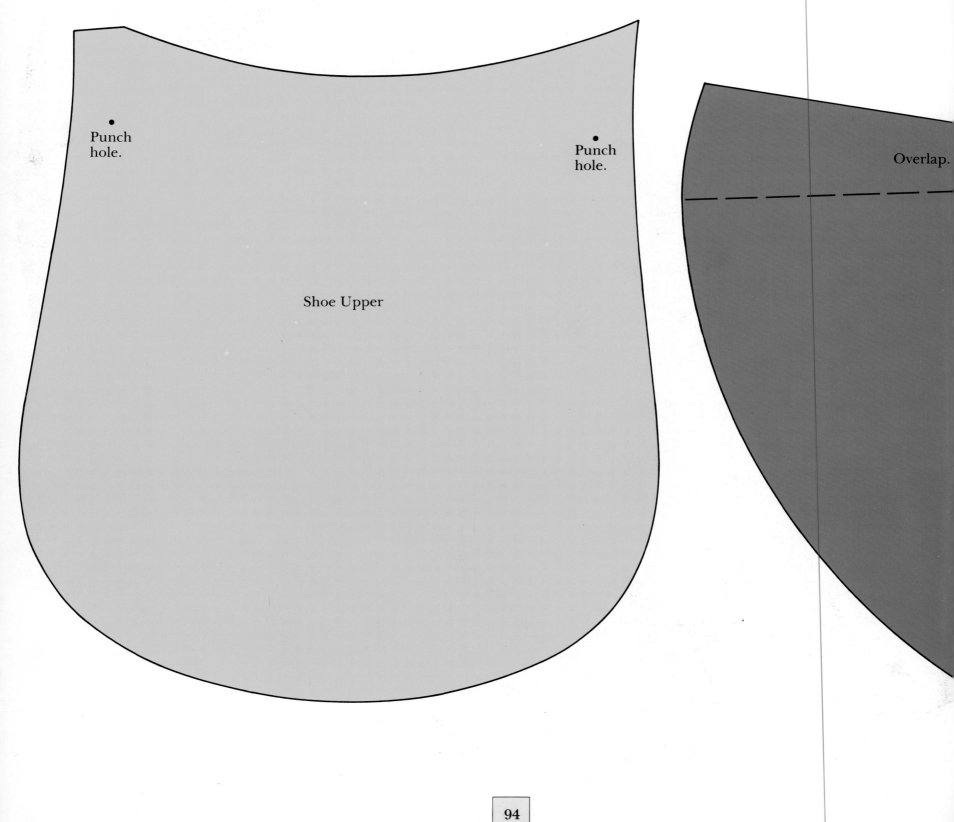

Punch
hole.

Punch
hole.

Shoe Upper

Overlap.

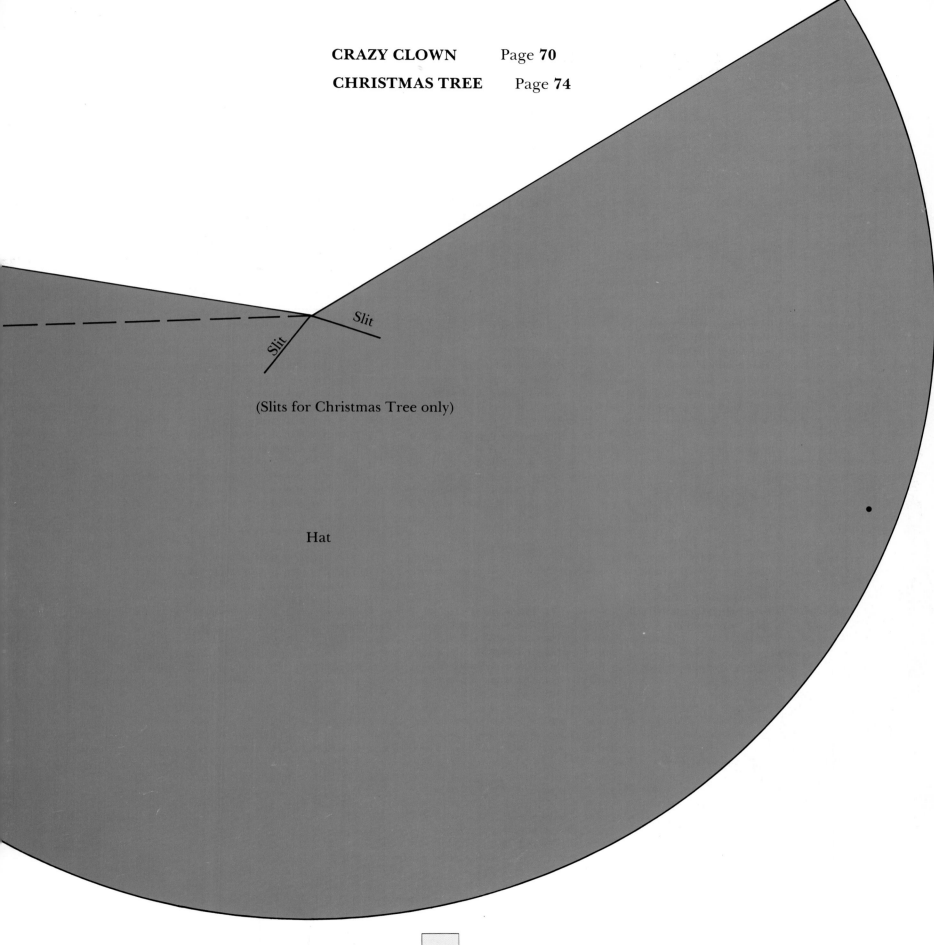

Slit

Slit

(Slits for Christmas Tree only)

Hat

INDEX

ACKNOWLEDGMENTS

The author and publishers would like to thank the following for their help in compiling this book:

Hallmark Cards Ltd.
Hallmark House
Station Road
Henley-on-Thames
Oxon RG9 1LQ
(Gift wrap and gift-wrap ribbons)

Forbo Mayfair
Station Road
Cramlington
Northumberland NE23 8AQ
(Sticky-backed plastic)

The Handicraft Shop
Northgate
Canterbury
Kent CT1 1BE
(Craft accessories)

Model Agencies
Kids Plus, 54 Grove Park,
London SE5 8LE
Scallywags, 1 Cranbrook Rise,
Ilford, Essex IG1 3QW
Tiny Tots, 9 Clifton Road,
London W9 1SZ